The Do-It-Yourself
PC Book

D1397956

Osborne/McGraw-Hill
A Division of the McGraw-Hill Companies

Published under licence from J H Haynes & Co Ltd, United Kingdom

© Haynes Publishing 2001. All rights reserved.

Printed in France by Pollina s.a., 85400 Luçon - n° L83890.

1 2 3 4 5 6 7 8 9 0

ISBN 0-07-213377-5

The Do-It-Yourself
PC Book

An Illustrated Guide to Upgrading and Repairing Your Computer

McGraw Hill **Osborne Media**

Contents

Introduction   **6**

① Getting to know your PC   **9**
A brief history of personal computing   10
Why upgrade?   14
Outside explained   16
Inside explained   18
Peripherals explained   20
Taking stock   22
Making an inventory   24
Taking precautions   26
The tools you'll need   31
Lifting the lid   33

② Boosting performance   **35**
Upgrading the processor – or not   36
Upgrading the motherboard – or not   42
Upgrading RAM   44

③ Adding a new drive   **49**
A word about channels   50
Why upgrade your hard disk drive?   52
Upgrading your CD-ROM drive   58
Adding a DVD drive   64
Floppy drive replacement   68
External drives   70

④ Expansion cards   **73**
A word about architecture   74
Upgrading your graphics card   76
Upgrading your sound card   80
Upgrading your modem   84
Adding USB   87

⑤ Peripheral devices   **91**
Upgrading your monitor   92
Upgrading your keyboard   97
Upgrading your mouse   100
Upgrading your speakers   102
Upgrading your printer   104
Upgrading your scanner   110

⑥ PC maintenance   **115**
Windows utilities   116
Third party utilities   122
Viruses – a special case   124
Taking precautions   126
Cleaning your PC   130

⑦ Trouble-shooting   **135**
Trouble-shooting in general   136
Trouble-shooting specific problems   138

⑧ Appendices   **143**
Appendix 1 Upgrade limitations   144
Appendix 2 BIOS and CMOS   145
Appendix 3 Partitioning your hard disk   147
Appendix 4 Glossary   149

Index   **154**

Acknowledgements   **158**

Introduction

Let's begin by asking two questions. Do you consider your home desktop computer system to be a fabulously powerful, immensely flexible, wholly essential and user-friendly tool? Or do you regard it as an overly complex, befuddling contraption, riddled with conflicting standards, prone to break down in any number of bizarre ways, instantly obsolete and bedevilled with an incomprehensible jargon developed by, and for, fully-fledged geeks?

Your answer to both questions is probably 'yes'. That's where we come in.

If you enjoy using your computer and want to make the most of your hardware (and your money) without becoming a dyed-in-the-wool techie in the process, this is the book for you. We'll show you in a series of clear step-by-step guides just how to upgrade, improve and enhance your system. We'll also consider how best to trouble-shoot problems and keep it all running smoothly. Above all, we'll endeavor to make everything easy.

Do please remember one thing: a computer is not like this year's model of a particular make of car. It's simply not possible for us to predict with any degree of certainty what's sitting on your desktop. Quite the reverse, in fact. The very essence and, indeed, appeal of the personal computer is that one size resolutely does not suit all: you can make of your system just what you will. This inevitably means that there are limitations to what we can cover here, and so our approach throughout is to focus on the most likely and common configurations.

The alternative – and there is only one – is to try to cover all angles, all bases, all permutations, all possible problems. What you end up with then is a massively unwieldy tome that ties itself in knots with cross-references and tables and endless ifs and buts … and still doesn't succeed in its aims.

No, we've striven instead to cover the basics and to give you enough background knowledge to tackle your own computer setup with confidence.

To that end, we're making certain assumptions here.

First, about you

You have a working (although not necessarily thorough) knowledge of Windows

You don't have an unlimited budget (or else you'd buy a brand new computer every 6 months and stay ahead of the game)

You're not scared to perform minor surgery on your computer (but you'd rather know what you're doing than fumble in the dark)

And secondly, about your computer

It has a Pentium processor or equivalent (definitely not an old 486, but probably not a shiny Pentium 4 either)

It's running Windows 95, 98 or Millennium Edition (not Windows 3.1)

It dates back no further than 1994/5

It has an internet connection (not essential but very, very helpful)

It's a PC, not a Mac!

Just a word on that last comment. Mac users are a sorely overlooked species in much computer literature. True, there aren't that many of them around, relatively speaking, despite the popular iMac, but that's no excuse. The real point is that a Mac has quite a different architecture to a PC and a significantly different operating system, and it's simply impractical, unhelpful and ultimately unfair to stick in the odd 'oh, and if you have a Mac, you might want to try this…' section in a book that deals primarily with PCs.

So we haven't. Rather, this is the manual for the discerning but probably somewhat frustrated owner of an 'average' Windows-based Pentium-powered PC. We can't promise to turn it into a supercomputer overnight but we certainly hope to help you prolong its lifespan and/or make it significantly better.

We keep the jargon to a minimum and practical guidance to the fore. After all, reading about computers is probably not high on your list of priorities, and upgrading, repairing and maintaining your hardware is not, with the best will in the world, what you might call fun. But using your computer is, or can and should be, and that's the point of this manual: to help ensure that your PC serves you well both now and in the future, however your needs may change.

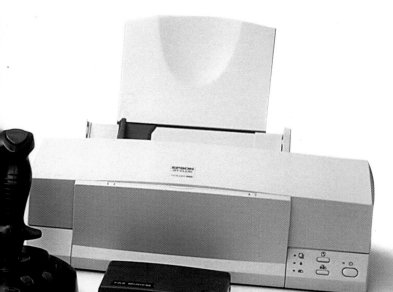

1

PART **1**

Getting to know your PC

A brief history of personal computing   **10**
Why upgrade?   **14**
Outside explained   **16**
Inside explained   **18**
Peripherals explained   **20**
Taking stock   **22**
Making an inventory   **24**
Taking precautions   **26**
The tools you'll need   **31**
Lifting the lid   **33**

First things first. Before we start poking around under the hood, let's take stock of your current computer setup. We're not exactly doing rocket science here but the best place to start is undoubtedly with a little basic background knowledge.

PART

A brief history of personal computing

It's become something of a cliché to claim that the Apollo moon missions were managed with less computing power than you'll find in today's typical car, electronic organizer, digital watch or musical greeting card… but it's true nonetheless. These days, everything from your coffeepot to your keyring carries a microchip and that bland, beige box stoically standing next to your desk is capable of performing more calculations in a split second than any mere mortal could achieve in a hundred lifetimes.

But it's a mistake to allow yourself to be overawed by technology. Always remember that a computer is a tool – no more and no less. It may be faster but you're smarter. (No, honestly, you are.) The chances are that you'll never *really* understand how your computer works, but so what? What counts is understanding how all the various bits and pieces work *together*. Grasp that and you'll soon be stripping, upgrading and rebuilding your PC before breakfast.

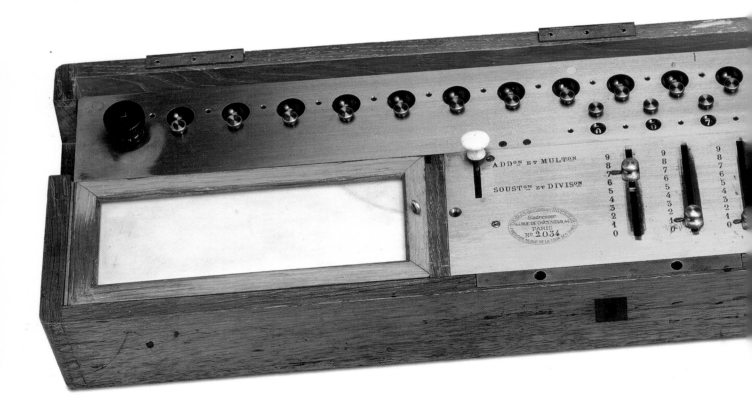

A functioning computer is essentially comprised of three parts

Hardware: *the motherboard, memory, processor, monitor, keyboard, modem, mouse and all the other nuts and bolts stuff.*

Operating system: *the master program that makes the hardware and software work together in perfect harmony (usually).*

Application software: *programs that let you do useful things with your PC like write letters, perform calculations, surf the internet and much, much more.*

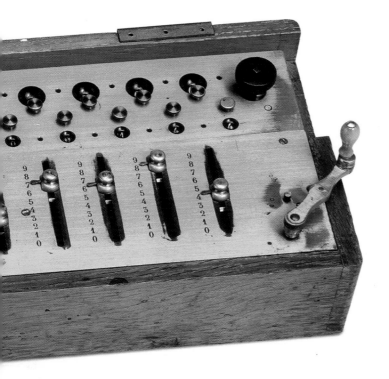

Charles X Thomas de Colmar invented his Arithmometer in 1820. It was the first commercially successful calculating machine and could be used for addition, subtraction, division and multiplication.

If you can get the distinction between hardware, the operating system and application software clear in your mind from the outset, then you've overcome one major hurdle. But if, for now, you don't know Windows from Word, ROM from RAM or a chipset from a chocolate chip, don't panic! You will, we promise.

So just how did we get here? Well, ask any two specialists about what really matters in the story of computing and you'll likely get two very different answers. But the one thing that they – and we – will agree upon is this: despite the checkered, convoluted and complex evolution of the personal computer, these days just about *anybody* can come to grips with the technology. What was once the exclusive province of geeks is now familiar territory to millions.

And that's a good thing. All you need is a little patience, a dash of logic, the confidence to tinker – and, of course, this manual as your guide.

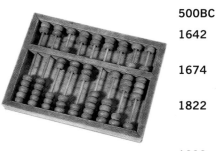

A Chinese abacus, the Suan Pan is the oldest form of abacus still in use.

Charles Babbage's Difference engine was finished in 1822. It was a decimal digital machine.

A controversial timeline

500BC   Ernie the Egyptian invents the abacus. Blame him

1642   Blaise Pascal invents an automatic adding machine of sorts

1674   Gottfried von Leibniz upgrades the Pascaline by adding multiplication

1822   Charles Babbage designs his Difference Engine, a mechanical calculator, but can't raise sufficient venture capital to build it

1833   Babbage upgrades his earlier invention to an Analytical Engine but doesn't build this one either

1890   Herman Hollerith comes up with a method for using punched cards to store data

1911   The Computing-Tabulating-Recording Company is founded in New York, and soon becomes IBM (International Business Machines)

1939   John Vincent Atanasoff and Clifford Berry invent the first true digital computer

1943   Alan Turing invents the *other* first true digital computer, Colossus, and uses it to crack the Germans' wartime Enigma code

1946   John Presper Eckert and John Mauchly develop ENIAC (Electronic Numerical Integrator And Computer), a fully-fledged computer replete with processor. It weighed in at 30 tons

1951   Eckert and Mauchly unveil UNIVAC (Universal Automatic Computer), the first computer to be sold commercially. It cost around $5million

1958   IBM develops a computer that uses transistors instead of vacuum tubes

1964   The integrated circuit is used for the first time in computer design

1965   Digital Equipment Corporation launches the first minicomputer, the PDP-8

1969   The US Department of Defense sets up a computer network called ARPANet (Advanced Research Projects Agency) that will one day become the internet

1970   The UNIX operating system is developed. So is the 8-inch floppy disk

1973   The first hard disk arrives courtesy of IBM: a 30MB monster with 16-inch platters called Winchester

The large disk is from an IBM system of 1984 and can hold 4MB, compared with the small hard disk from 1999 which can hold 6GB!

The Altair 8800b microcomputer of 1975.

'PalmPilot' palmtop computer of 1998. Manufactured by US Robotics.

1975 The Altair 8800 – the first microcomputer, or PC – is sold to the public. It cost $400 and you had to build it yourself. Bill Gates and Paul Allen found Microsoft to sell software for it

1976 Steve Jobs and Steve Wozniak found Apple Computer

1978 The 5.25 inch floppy disk becomes the (temporary) standard medium for portable, removable storage.

1980 British inventor Clive Sinclair launches the kit-form ZX-80 computer. Sales of soldering irons soar and a generation of geeks is born. Ready-assembled model launched a month later to wicked and unsubstantiated rumours that they were customer-assembled models returned to Sinclair for repair.

1981 The IBM PC hits the streets. The 3.5 inch floppy disk also makes its first appearance

1982 The PC wins Time Magazine's 'Man of the Year' and the Sinclair ZX Spectrum brings computer games to the mass market

1984 Apple introduces the Macintosh computer. It uses a mouse and clickable icons and menus

1985 The first commercial version of Windows is launched by Microsoft

1988 Apple sues Microsoft for copying the graphical look and feel of its operating system. Then again, Apple allegedly pinched the idea from Xerox

1991 Tim Berners-Lee invents the World Wide Web. Physicists at the nuclear lab CERN in Switzerland (where Berners-Lee worked) wonder what good it is

1994 Jeff Bezos quits Wall Street and decides to start an internet bookstore, Amazon.com

1995 Microsoft introduces Windows 95, which looks suspiciously like the Apple Mac. People suddenly find PCs easy to use, sales skyrocket, and Bill Gates becomes rather rich

1996 Microsoft introduces Internet Explorer and sets off a browser war with Netscape, ultimately making web browsing software free – and the web ever more interesting to freeloaders

1999 The World Wide Web becomes the hottest thing on Wall Street. Millionaires are created as fast as you can say IPO

2000 Web businesses lead technology stocks to all-time highs, then crash taking technology with it

2001 In the wake of the crash, PC and peripheral prices fall and make computer hardware the best buy ever – which means there's no better time than today to upgrade

PART 1 — Why upgrade?

Back in 1965, a rising young engineer called Gordon Moore (who went on to co-found Intel) noted that computers had a habit of doubling in power every 18 months or so. His observation came to be enshrined as 'Moore's Law' and remarkably still holds true today. Ironically, we long ago passed the point where we actually *need* more computing power in our homes and offices, and yet still we rush lemming-like to upgrade or replace hardware that's barely out of warranty. Why?

Because I can? No, no, no... that's the answer of an inveterate geek. Now there's nothing wrong with being an inveterate geek – well, okay, there is, but we won't go into that here – but if you're the type to fix things that positively ain't broke, this ain't the book for you.

Because I want to? Really? You get kicks from tinkering with hardware? *Really?* There's certainly much satisfaction to be had from fixing or improving a PC but we'd draw the line at calling it fun.

Because I must? Absolutely. This is the only time when it makes true sense to upgrade your PC. There are, in fact, three quite distinct (good) reasons to upgrade:

Three good reasons to upgrade

To improve performance This is when your existing setup simply isn't up to the demands placed upon it, often as a result of changes in your own work or play habits. A system purchased for bookkeeping and business letters is unlikely to cut the mustard at 3-D gaming.

While performance-enhancing upgrades can significantly prolong the lifespan of your PC, it's important to make the *right* upgrades. As we go along, we'll consider which upgrades are practicable and worthwhile – and when it's better to admit defeat, throw the whole system in the trash and start afresh with a brand new computer!

To repair a broken component Unfortunately, unless you're a wiz with a soldering iron, your chances of actually repairing anything are slim indeed. You *could* take a can opener to a stalled hard disk or hotwire a sound card... but we wouldn't advise it. No, the fact is that when something breaks down, it almost always need replacing – and in such cases it's easy to make a virtue of necessity by installing something altogether better. Why replace an ancient, slow CD-ROM drive with a not-so-slow CD-ROM drive when you could just as easily fit a shiny new CD-Recordable or Rewriteable drive instead, thereby simultaneously effecting a repair, boosting performance *and* adding new functionality?

To add new features Want to play DVD movies on your PC? Need a backup device? Run out of hard disk space? Craving a bigger monitor or better printer? These are examples of upgrading a system by adding things that are currently lacking. Again, we'll look at all the options.

Repairing and enhancing a PC are all good reasons for minor surgery.

But before we get carried away, let's consider two further questions

Do you need really *need* to upgrade? Please understand that we're not trying to discourage you from upgrading your PC – quite the reverse – but there are times when a little sober reflection can pay dividends and save you money. For instance, is your software placing unnecessary demands on your hardware? Do you really need that full-blown, memory-hogging monolithic office suite just to balance the household budget? Would it be worthwhile buying a dedicated games console instead of converting your dusty old computer to a lean, mean fighting/driving/flying machine? Is your hard disk clogged with seldom-used programs that could be easily deleted to free up space? And would simply defragmenting your hard disk make a world of difference to your PC's performance?

If much of this sounds deeply mysterious right now, don't panic! We'll cover all the angles in detail soon enough. But if you're contemplating an upgrade simply because your once fleet of foot system is now limping lamely, jump straight to the Maintenance section on page 115. A little rudimentary house-keeping can work wonders – and save you a bundle.

***Can* you upgrade?** A recent trend in computer design has made it easier (arguably) to get up and running with a PC straight out of the box. Often integrated multimedia circuitry replaces expansion cards, which means that it's nearly impossible to add a new graphics or sound card if and when your needs change. In some cases, such as Compaq's business-oriented iPaq, it's difficult to get at the inside components at all. The thinking is that you can only get into trouble tinkering around inside, that you can do whatever expansion you need to through new external interfaces such as USB and FireWire ports. Opt for one of these machines, and upgrades are off-limits. You're stuck with what you've bought no matter how wonderfully technology improves.

One day, perhaps, all PCs will be made this way. One day, perhaps, PCs will be ten for a dollar and it'll be cheaper to buy a new one than fuss around with upgrades and repairs. One day, perhaps, PCs will be genuinely easy to use. And one day, just perhaps, the PC will cease to exist in anything like its current shape and form.

But not today, and probably not tomorrow. For now, millions of us own computer systems that are teetering on the edge of obsolescence but not quite ready for the landfill. This is the manual for people who can use a screwdriver but not a soldering iron; people who won't throw good money after bad but don't want to buy a new computer unless and until they absolutely have to; and people who are allergic to acronyms.

PART **1** **Outside explained**

CD-ROM drive *A compact disc player that handles multimedia CDs as well as the plain audio CD format. With most CD-ROM drives, a flat tray pops out and sucks the disc into the machine. Note that DVD, CD-R and CD-RW drives look identical to CD-ROM drives, and use the same 5.25 inch drive bay.*

Floppy drive *Floppy disks are a stalwart form of removable media. But while they may be cheap, the drives are sluggish and capacity is limited to 1.44 MB per disk.*

Reset switch *When Windows freezes and all else fails, this button restarts the system. Not one to push in error.*

Power LED *This light lets you know your computer is switched on, just in case the fan wasn't loud enough to clue you in.*

Drive Activity LED *A light that flashes when you read or write data from your hard disk as a reassurance all is well.*

On/off switch *Does just what you'd expect. Of course, you know better than to switch off a PC without first going through the proper Windows shut down procedure, don't you (bizarre though it may be to press a Start button to stop the operating system)?*

Case *The majority of PCs now come in tower format (tall and narrow) rather than desktop (flat and wide). There are various standards governing case design, related to the size and shape of the motherboard within. If you were building a PC from scratch, this would be your first concern. But you're not, so it's not.*

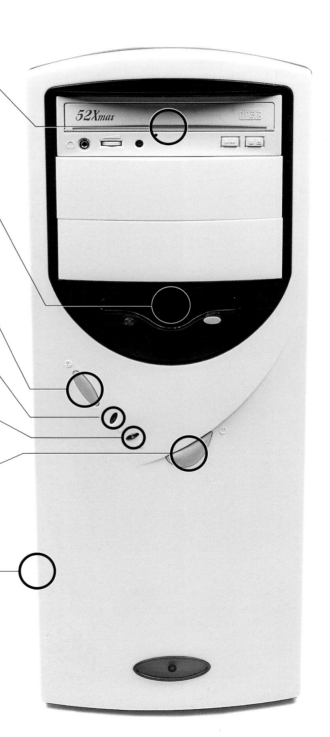

Power switch *If present (don't worry if it's not), this switch controls the internal power supply.*

Keyboard and mouse ports *Six-pin female sockets (formerly called mini-DIN jacks): on newer PCs coded green for the mouse, pale purple for the keyboard. Old systems may use a larger 5-pin DIN jack for the keyboard. You can also plug a mouse into a serial port, although the computer industry eventually wants both your mouse and keyboard to slide into USB ports.*

Serial port *A 9-pin male socket commonly used to connect external modems and older mice. One or two such ports are the norm, known to Windows as COM1 and COM2, though legacy-free new PCs may omit them, too.*

Monitor connector *A 15-pin female socket used to connect the monitor. This is the visible end of the internal graphics adapter. Depending upon the capabilities of the card, there may also be an array of video outputs.*

Modem connector *If the PC has an internal modem, there will be a modular jack (usually a four-pin jack formerly known as RJ-11) to connect it to the telephone system via a cable. Alternatively, your PC may have an Ethernet card onboard, in which case there will be an 8-pin RJ-45 socket.*

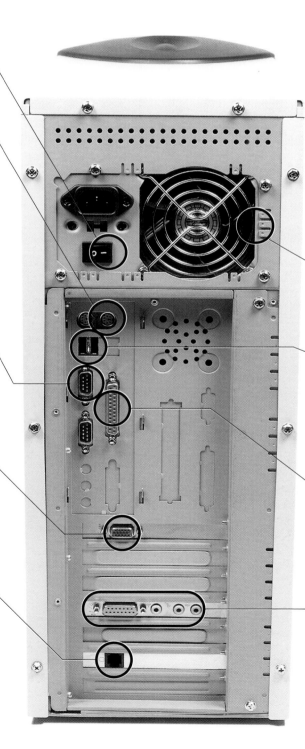

Cooling fan *Air inlet for the internal fan. Without suitable cooling, a PC would soon get hot enough to fry an egg. And its own circuitry.*

USB ports *Newer sockets generally not found on PCs built before 1997/8. Faster and more flexible than either the parallel or serial port, USB (Universal Serial Bus) is becoming the de facto standard for connecting external devices.*

Parallel port *A 25-pin female socket commonly used to connect a printer, although some new systems omit it in favor of USB printers. Windows refers to this port as LPT1.*

Audio connectors *A PC fitted with a sound card will typically have one or two outlets for speakers and perhaps jacks for connecting a microphone and other audio equipment. It may also have a game port designed for a joystick.*

PART  # Inside explained

We don't suggest for a minute that you dive straight to the innards of your PC but we're going to be talking a lot about motherboards, components and expansion cards as we go on. Here's a sneak preview of what to expect under the hood.

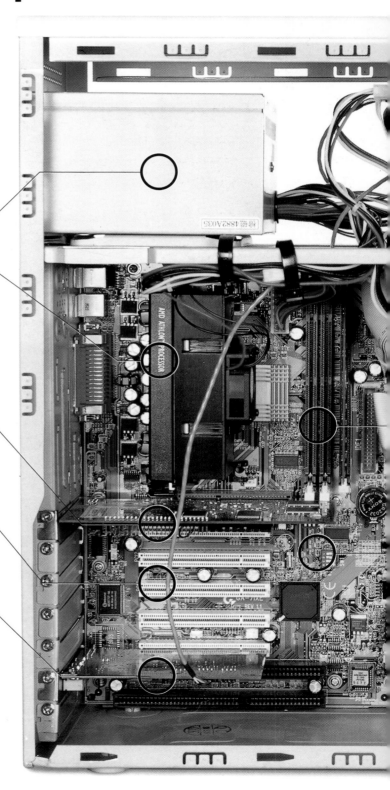

Power supply *A metal-cased assembly that converts AC utility power into the special low voltages required by your computer's circuitry*

Processor *Usually thought of as the brains of a computer, the processor does number crunching on a grand scale. Chances are you'll have either an Intel or an AMD processor onboard – perhaps a Cyrix in an older system or a Transmeta Crusoe in a new one – sitting either in a socket mounting (flat on the motherboard) or in a slot (on edge). The odds are it'll be hidden under a fan or a spiky metal heatsink to keep it cool.*

Graphics card *The graphics card is a printed circuit board responsible for producing the images that you see on your monitor screen. It's possible to build the circuitry right into the motherboard but this is an example of an expansion card (discussed in detail on p.74).*

Free expansion slots *These special spaces inside your computer provide a place and socket for adding new capabilities to your computer. In modern computers, these are often called PCI slots.*

Sound card *Circuitry that's sometimes another expansion card and sometimes part of the motherboard that, as you might expect, controls the PC's sound capability. Note the lead linking the sound card to the CD-ROM drive. This enables the card to pick up the soundtrack on an audio CD or CD-ROM and broadcast it through speakers or headphones.*

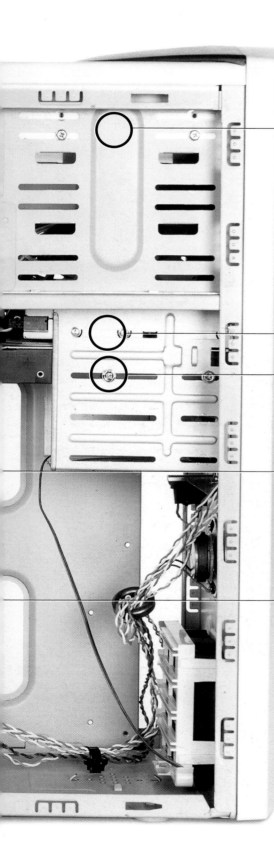

CD-ROM drive *A refugee from your stereo system, the CD drive in your computer lets you load new software and play music discs. Newer systems have drives that let you make your own CDs.*

Floppy drive *This dinosaur bit of technology once was the best way to add programs to your computer and save files. Today it's there because it's always been there.*

Hard disk *The hard disk is a device that permanently stores data until such time as you decide to delete or modify it. Every time you hit the Save button in a word processor, for instance, the document you're working on is copied to the hard disk, so it's safe even if the power is suddenly switched off. The process of saving data is called* writing to the hard disk; *retrieving it is* reading from the hard disk.

Memory *Random Access Memory, or RAM. It comes as small circuit boards called memory modules that sit in rows of sockets on the motherboard. RAM is a temporary working space in which the PC's business is conducted from moment to moment.*

Motherboard *A great big printed circuit board. You really can't miss it because everything else plugs into it one way or another. Think of it as your PC's nervous system – a series of channels and conduits transmitting information from any one part of the system to any other. If you don't have a computer from a major brand with good on-line support, getting hold of the manual that came with your motherboard is going to save a lot of headaches and uncertainty later.*

TECHIE CORNER

Drive Bays A drive bay is a space in the case of a PC into which a drive may be installed. For reasons too dull to discuss, two sizes evolved, as shown here. Floppy and desktop hard disk drives use the 3.5-inch standard, notebook hard disks fit a tighter 2.5-inch bay and virtually everything else the 5.25-inch standard. Note that the latter is also referred to as a half-height drive, so don't panic if you come across the term: a CD writer will fit just fine

Drive bay	3.5"	5.25"
Actual width	4"	5.75"
Actual depth	5.75"	8"
Actual height	1"	1.63"

PART

Peripherals explained

The items on these pages are examples of what are commonly referred to as peripherals. You might be surprised to find the monitor comes under this heading – after all, you can't do much with a PC without one – but the hard disk is also, strictly speaking, a peripheral device. That is, a computer is still technically a computer without a storage device, a display unit or input devices. What it patently is not is useful! That's where peripherals come in: they let you do exciting, fun, useful stuff with your computer.

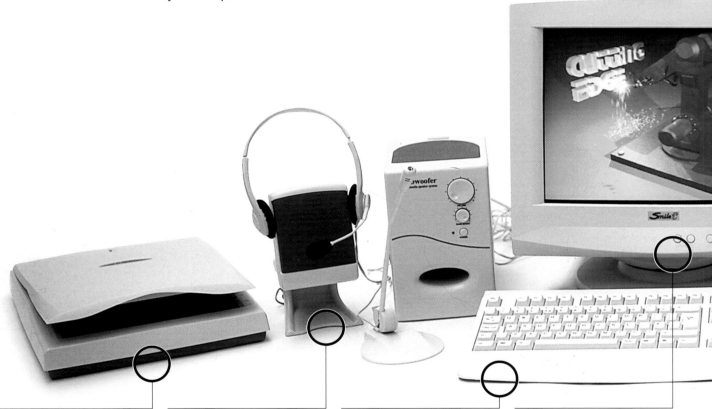

Scanner *Scanners turn documents and pictures into digital images which you can then view and play with on the PC. Strictly optional but rather useful.*

Speakers *These range from cheap, tinny and worthless to quite extraordinarily powerful. They plug into your computer's sound card.*

Keyboard *A dumb typewriter renowned for accumulating crumbs and other debris. It translates the motion of your fingers pressing keys into digital codes that your computer interprets as numbers, letters, and commands.*

Monitor *A display screen housed within a big, deep, bulky box – or, if it's modern, perhaps a smaller, flatter, less bulky box.*

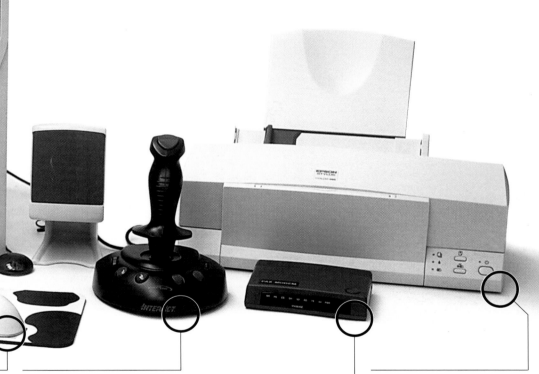

Mouse Small plastic clickable rodent that lives on a mat. The premiere pointing device, the mouse allows you to issue commands and move objects without typing.

Joystick Worthwhile to get the most out of computer games.

Modem Essential equipment for accessing the internet or sending paperless faxes. A modem translates computer data into sounds that can be sent down a standard phone line to other computers. Many PCs come with modems pre-installed internally on an expansion card, but stand-alone units are also available (and much easier to manage). A DSL router or cable modem serves the same purpose as the modem but provides higher speed – often called "broadband" – access to the internet.

Printer Despite the dream of a paperless office, hard copies of documents still have a place in most of our lives. The printer turns your computer's fleeting thoughts into such hard copy, nowadays with photo-like color.

PART  Taking stock

If you've ever bought off-the-shelf software, you'll know that there's usually a panel on the box stating the "minimum system requirements." Along the lines of:

IBM PC or 100% compatible computer
Intel Pentium II 266MHz or higher processor
Windows 95, 98, ME or XP
96 MB of RAM (128 MB recommended)
500 MB free hard disk space
CD-ROM drive
Monitor 256-colors SVGA or better
Sound card
Internet connection

But what does it all mean? And does your PC come up to scratch? That's one problem; another crops up when you come to go shopping for upgrade components. You see, you can't just go buy a bit more RAM without knowing what *kind* of RAM you need. And how much. And whether there's space for it on the motherboard.

The good news is if you start off with a thorough inventory of your current system, you really can't go far wrong. First of all, dig out the paperwork that came with your new PC. Here, you should find all the main specifications clearly laid out. However, that's only going to get you so far (and, of course, it's highly possible that you no longer have or simply can't find the original documentation). Thus we turn to Windows.

Check the minimum system requirements before you splash out on software

Device advice

Click Start.
Click Settings.
Click Control Panel.

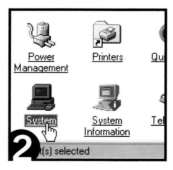

Double click System icon.

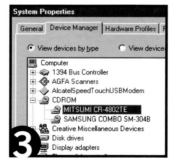

Click the Device Manager tab. (In Windows 2000, you'll have to hit the Hardware tab first, then the Device Manager button). Now, just by using Device Manager, you can investigate your entire hardware setup at a glance. Click the + sign alongside any component to see more detail. In this example, we've expanded the CD-ROM section and can see that there are two drives installed (one made by Mitsumi, the other by Samsung).

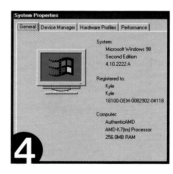

Next, click the General tab to see how much RAM is inside your PC – in this case, 256MB. We can also see that the processor is an AMD model.

Speed trap

Curiously, you won't find any mention of your processor's speed, although you should see it appear briefly if you watch the monitor screen carefully when you first start your PC. Not convinced? Then download and run the following utilities:
For an Intel processor:
http://support.intel.com/support/processors/tools/frequencyid/download.htm
For an AMD processor: **http://www.amd.com/products/cpg/bin/cpuinfo.exe**

Unfortunately, and unhelpfully, the Intel version does not work with processors earlier than the Pentium III range. In this case, download the free version of Sandra (System ANalyser, Diagnostic and Reporting Assistant) and run the CPU & BIOS module: **http://www.sisoftware.co.uk/sandra**

In fact, Sandra's many tools will tell you just about everything you'll ever need to know about your system – hardware, software, technical configurations – and it's easier to use and clearer than Windows' own tools. The commercial version (US $29 at the time of writing) has 70 separate modules that between them cover every base. Another useful package is Norton Utilities 2001 from Symantec (US $49.95): **http://www.symantec.com/nu/nu_9x/**

Easy, isn't it? But what's alarming is the realization that this information is only readily accessible when Windows is working. What if it's not? What if your processor starts shooting sparks or you need to replace the hard disk? May we therefore suggest that you take a few minutes now to print out your device manager display. Better still, complete the more-detailed table on the following pages. Don't worry if you can't fill in all the blanks.

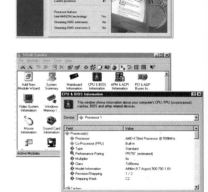

Software utilities make it simple to see just what your system is made of.

Rooting around

In Windows 98 and later versions (including ME and 2000), another non-surgical route to the heart of your system is the System Information tool:
Click Start.
Click Programs.
Click Accessories.
Click System Tools.
Click System Information.

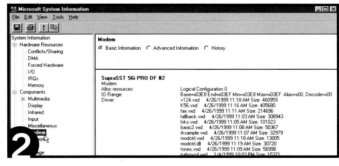

Again, click the + signs to see details of your system. Be sure to select the Basic Information option. Different versions of Windows may have their own look, but they provide much the same information.

Making an inventory

Component	For instance...	Your system	Notes
PC Manufacturer/model	Dell Dimension		Should be printed on the front of the case
PC Serial number	D123456		Printed or stamped on the back of case
Case	ATX		The 'form factor' matches the motherboard description (check the manual)
Operating system	Windows 98		Look in the General tab of System Properties (or use Sandra)
Processor manufacturer	Intel, AMD, Cyrix		Look in the General tab of System Properties (or use Sandra)
Processor model	Pentium II, Duron		See comments about using the manufacturer's utility or Sandra on p.23
Processor speed	266MHz		See comments about using the manufacturer's utility or Sandra on p.23
BIOS manufacturer/version	Award version 6		BIOS information is displayed briefly onscreen when you first start your PC. Alternatively, use the BIOS module in Sandra
Quantity of RAM	64MB		Look in the General tab of System Properties (or use Sandra)
Type of RAM	SIMM, DIMM		If this is not clear from the original paperwork, use the Mainboard Information module in Sandra
Hard disk capacity	3GB		Click My Computer, click with the right mouse button on C:, and select Properties from the menu
Hard disk interface	IDE, SCSI, UDMA 33, UDMA 66, UDMA 100		Look under Disk Drives in Device Manager (or use Sandra)
Floppy disk size	3.5 inch, 5.25 inch		Click My Computer, click with the right mouse button on A:, and select Properties from the menu
CD-ROM drive manufacturer	Matsushita CR585		Look in Device Manager (or use Sandra)
CD-ROM drive speed	24x		Check the documentation or look on the front of the case

Fill in as much information as you can about your current computer. It's a valuable exercise that will pay dividends later.

Component	For instance...	Your system	Notes
Drive letter assigned to CD-ROM	D:		Look in My Computer
Other drive details	Zip, DVD		If your PC has other installed drives, note what you can about them here
Spare 5.25 inch drive bays	2		Look for blank plastic covers on the front of the case, probably just under the CD-ROM drive
Spare 3.5 inch drive bays	1		Ditto, but don't be surprised to find none. 3.5 inch drive bays are sometimes accessible only from inside the case
Monitor manufacturer/model	Taxan Ergovision		Printed or stamped on the monitor case
Monitor size	15 inch		This is the screen size measured diagonally from corner to corner. See p92 for details
Monitor type	CRT, LCD		See p.92
Modem type	Internal or external		If you plug your telephone cable directly into a socket around the back of your PC, you've got an internal modem!
Modem speed/standard	56Kbps, v90		See p.84
Graphics card	ATi RagePro		Look under Display Adapters in Device Manager (or use Sandra)
Sound card details	SoundBlaster Live		Look under Sound, Video and Games Controllers in Device Manager (or use Sandra)
Additional installed expansion cards	FireWire card, Ethernet adapter		Look in Device Manager (or use Sandra)
Printer manufacturer/model	HP LaserJet 1100		Click Start, Settings and Printers
Printer type	Inkjet, laser		See p.104
Scanner manufacturer/model	Agfa SnapScan 310		Look in Device Manager (or use Sandra)
Scanner type	Flatbed, sheet fed		See p.110
Other peripherals	Joystick, speakers		Look in Device Manager (or use Sandra)

PART  Taking precautions

Before turning another page, and certainly before taking a screwdriver to your computer, ask yourself these questions:
How would I cope if my PC refused to restart?
How would I cope if my files became corrupted?
How would I cope if my PC was stolen?
Temporary inconvenience or a major catastrophe? If your computer went badly awry, would you lose a day's work, a week's work, or the sum total of your efforts over the past year?

Safe or sorry?

It's important to recognize the difference between a computer failure and the loss of data. In the case of a software problem, it's usually possible to reinstall Windows (and any of your programs that you need to) from scratch. Tedious, but possible, and with luck all your documents and files will survive. However, a better idea is to take precautionary measures now, and that means making a startup disk. This way, you can start your PC even if your hard disk won't boot. At the very least, you should be able to make emergency copies of your files before taking more drastic (and dangerous) action, such as re-installing Windows.

Losing data is an altogether more serious proposition. No matter how careful you are, *any* computer upgrade, repair or maintenance carries with it a risk of damage. The only sensible approach – and believe us, we speak from hard and bitter experience – is to make backup copies of all your important files. In fact, make multiple copies, do it regularly, and keep them somewhere safe (and safe does not mean in your desk drawer: it means in an entirely different location, ideally in a fireproof box hidden under somebody else's floorboards!). There's a good chance that you made a Windows startup disk (or rescue, emergency or boot disk – they're all one and the same thing) when you first bought or acquired your computer. There's a higher chance still that you've since misplaced it, so let's make a fresh one now. Just follow these step-by-step instructions.

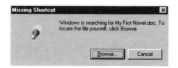

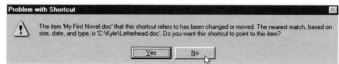

Lost files are at best a headache but can sometimes prove disastrous.

Making a Windows 98 and newer startup disk

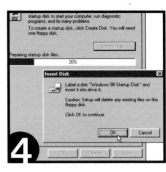

First, insert a blank floppy disk in its drive
Click Start.
Click Settings.
Click Control Panel.

Double-click *the Add/Remove Programs icon.*

Click *the Startup Disk tab.*

Click *Create Disk.*

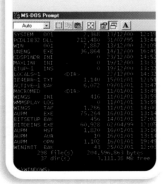

That's it. To test the disk, leave it in its drive and restart your PC. Instead of seeing the familiar Windows screen – remember, this is for emergencies when Windows itself is in need of repair – the computer will stay in DOS-mode and give you the option to start it up with or without CD-ROM support. Select the 'with support' option. Slide a disc into your CD drive, and when you see a blinking A:\> prompt, type D: and press enter (assuming that D: is the drive letter usually assigned to your CD-ROM drive). You should get a D:\> prompt. Type dir and press Enter. If you can see a list of the files on the disc, congratulations. You could now reinstall Windows from the original CD-ROM (which you do, of course, still have safe, right?). In the meantime, remove the floppy disk from its drive, label it Startup Disk, and press the reset switch. Windows will now start as normal.

Making a Windows 95 startup disk

Oh dear. It all gets a bit messy now. The problem is that Windows 95 startup disks do not include drivers for the CD-ROM drive. In other words, although the disk will start the system and allow you to carry out rudimentary repair work (if you know how), there's no way to access the CD-ROM drive. What *this* means is that you can't reinstall Windows because that requires access to, er, the CD-ROM drive. Not brilliant, is it?

The solution is to locate a DOS driver for your CD-ROM drive and include it on the startup disk. If you're lucky, and if you've kept everything that shipped with the original equipment, you may find a floppy disk helpfully labelled 'this is a DOS driver for your CD-ROM drive'. But what are the chances of that happening?

One approach is to establish who made the drive by looking in Device Manager, as described earlier. Make a note of the model. Now track down the company's website and look for a driver download area. Be sure to look for a DOS driver, not a Windows driver (which is quite different and useless in the present circumstances). Alternatively, try the following websites:

http://www.drivershq.com
http://www.windrivers.com
http://www.driverzone.com

Once you have located and/or downloaded the appropriate driver, make a startup disk as described above. The procedure may vary slightly depending upon which version of Windows 95 you have. When that's done, copy the DOS driver onto the floppy disk.

Unfortunately, at this point you also have to manually edit some critical system files on the disk, and this is when it all gets horribly complicated. For the clearest walkthrough of the process around, visit Bob O'Donnell's page here:

http://www.everythingcomputers.com/windows_boot_disk.htm

This site is also worth a visit, and it includes a file download to get your startup disk working with generic CD drives:

http://www.fixwindows.com/win95/cdboot.htm

Better still, upgrade to a newer version of Windows. Stepping up to 98 will end the startup silliness! Windows ME not only cleans up the startup nonsense but will make your system boot faster, and XP will give you the same added reliability you get from the "professional" version, Windows 2000.

Backing up your files

How you make copies of your valuable files depends largely upon your system. That is, if you have nothing but a floppy drive onboard, you're pretty well limited to shifting data in batches of 1.44MB or less (which equates to around 700 disks per gigabyte!). Zip and SuperDisk drives, by contrast, use disks with capacities of 100 to 250MB, depending on the model, and a recordable CD drive lets you backup 650MB of data at a time (and quickly too). A tape drive offers even greater flexibility. Indeed, one of the best reasons for upgrading a PC is to improve your options for backing up data.

Do bear in mind the difference between backups and archives. Backing up your current company accounts onto a Zip disk and keeping it in a fire-proof safe protects you if your office burns down. Archiving data, on the other hand, is making a copy of information you want to hang on to but rarely need to use. Burning last year's accounts onto a CD-R means you can put the disk on the shelf and delete the file from your PC, freeing up space.

Getting your backup

One method is simply to copy your files onto a floppy or Zip disk using Windows Explorer or My Computer. Recordable CD-ROMs (CD-R and CD-RW discs) work slightly differently. Nearly all new writeable CD drives include software that lets you copy files from hard disk to CD. With packet-writing software (which some but not all CD drives include) you can move files to CD as easily as you move them around your hard disk, simply dragging them with your mouse.

Alternatively, there are plenty of utility software programs around that automate the backup process. Some will even save your files to a floppy or Zip disk on the fly as you work.

Recordable compact discs are a cheap and efficient way to archive your old data.

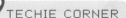

Windows 98 comes with its own utility called, unsurprisingly, Microsoft Backup. If it's already installed on your PC, you'll find it by clicking Start, Programs, Accessories and System Tools. If it's not there, open the Add/Remove Programs dialog box (see p.27), click on the Windows Setup tab, and install Backup in the System Tools section. You'll need your original Windows CD-ROM disk.

The beauty of Backup is that it supports disk spanning, which means that a backup job gets saved seamlessly across as many floppy (or Zip) disks as necessary. In other words, you can select as many files for backing up as you want to without worrying about their sizes: the program automatically asks for the requisite number of disks and saves the data piecemeal fashion.

Restoring data is essentially just a case of running Backup in reverse and inserting the floppy disks *in the right order* when prompted (which adds up to one very good reason for labelling them properly as you make the original backup!)

However, some important caveats: the Windows 95 version of Backup does *not* support removable drives like Zip or tape. See this web-page for details:

http://support.microsoft.com/support/kb/articles/Q135/2/80.asp?
LN=EN-GB&SD=gn&FR=0

The Windows 98 version might not initially offer to use your Zip or tape drive, but it can be persuaded to do so. See:

http://support.microsoft.com/support/kb/articles/Q186/1/68.ASP?
LN=EN-GB&SD=gn&FR=0

and:

http://support.microsoft.com/support/kb/articles/Q188/5/75.ASP?
LN=EN-GB&SD=gn&FR=0

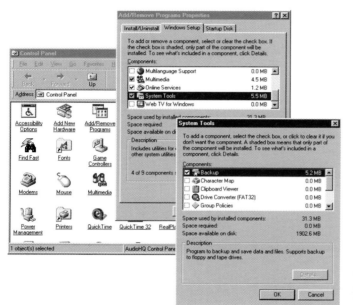

Backup is an optional extra in Windows but easily installed from the CD-ROM.

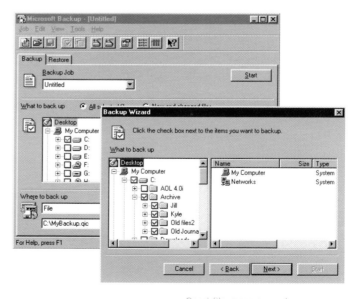

Good file management pays dividends when it comes to backing up your data.

PART 1

The tools you'll need

As we remarked earlier, fiddling with computers isn't rocket science. Nor is it brain surgery. It's a whole lot easier than replacing a car's suspension, or even the brakes on a bicycle, and it requires neither skill nor experience. Short of spilling your coffee over the motherboard, you're very unlikely to actually break your computer. However, do give yourself plenty of space to work. For even the simplest internal task, it's worthwhile shifting the whole shebang from a cramped desktop to somewhere more suitable. At the very least, ensure that you have sufficient room to work comfortably with a tower PC lying on its side.

If you can change a fuse, you can upgrade a computer.

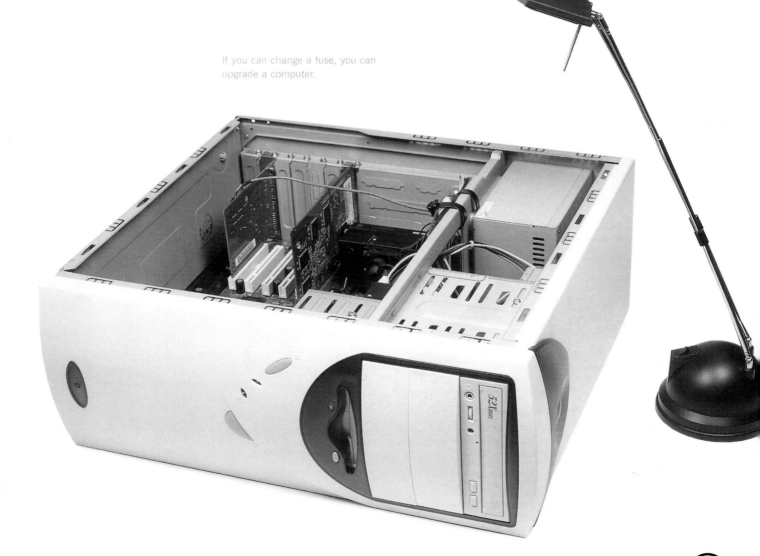

You'll need five tools to work on your PC's delicate innermost parts

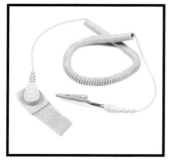

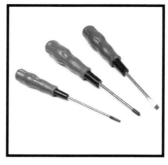

A manual for your motherboard and, ideally, all the other manuals and paperwork that came with your PC and peripherals. The non-technical manuals that come with major computer brands usually have the essential information you need for upgrading. If your motherboard is a mystery, however, download a copy of Sandra (see p.23) and run the Mainboard module. Now visit the manufacturer's website and cross your fingers that there's a downloadable manual available.

An antistatic wrist-strap It won't save your life if you upgrade a running PC from the comfort of your bath but it will disperse any build-up of static electricity in your body and thus safeguard delicate circuitry from an unwelcome fry-up. Your computer will thank you for it – and so will your wallet. Wear one with pride. No one we know actually uses one, but our lawyers say we'd better recommend it so if something breaks while you're upgrading, it's your fault not ours.

Screwdrivers One small Phillips will probably suffice – that's the one with the cross-shaped pointy end – but have a flathead screwdriver at hand just in case. Most PCs use hex-headed screws that allow you to use a nut-driver to twist out those almost welded in place. If you can't resist, buy one of those handy 'PC upgrade' kits. You'll get nut drivers, screwdrivers, and a bunch of odd little pieces that you can pretend are useful.

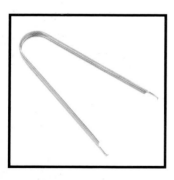

There's only one other must-have, and that's patience. Always a virtue, a measure of patience is truly essential when it comes to upgrading a PC. The task at hand might not be successful at the first attempt. You might have trouble installing drivers or any one of a million minor problems may strike without warning. But don't rush it. Ever. Take your time, work through the manual that comes with any new device or component (even if it's written in Jargonese, as is the norm), and think logically. Don't replace your hard disk on a Monday morning or network the office on a Friday afternoon when you'd rather be elsewhere. There. Now are you ready to peek inside?

Tweezers or delicate long-nosed pliers. Essential for retrieving dropped screws.

A flashlight Miniaturization ensures a surfeit of nooks and crannies inside your computer, and they're all dark.

PART 1 Lifting the lid

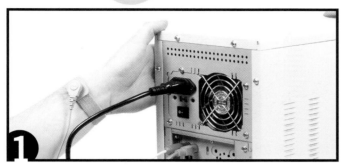

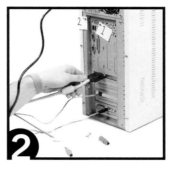

Opinions vary on whether it's safer to leave the PC's case connected to the mains while you work – with the power turned off at the wall, of course. This provides a path to a ground for static electricity and protects the computer's components. That's the approach that we'll adopt here. However, do feel free to unplug the machine completely if it makes you more comfortable – and certainly do this if there's no on/off switch at your wall socket.

Unplug all other cables and connectors from the back of the machine. If it helps, make a note of where everything goes, perhaps using sticky labels. In practice, thanks to myriad different interfaces present on the back of your PC, the plug on the end of a peripheral's cable will typically fit only one socket.

Dig out the manual that came with your computer and figure out what holds it together. Yes, we know that sounds rather vague but there are any number of ways to screw a case together, and few of them are obvious. We've even seen a design where to get at the retaining screws you have to forcibly pry off the front of the case. Talk about counter-intuitive!

Touch something metal to discharge any static electricity in your body. Before going near anything internally, put on your wrist-strap and connect it to a metal part of the case. Now peer inside. Does it look like the picture on the right? Good. Then it's definitely a computer. Now let's make it a better one.

PART  # Boosting performance

Upgrading the processor – or not   **36**

Upgrading the motherboard – or not   **42**

Upgrading RAM   **44**

You'd think, would you not, that the quickest way to speed up an ailing PC would be to give it a brainpower boost? Surprisingly, this isn't always – indeed, not even usually – the case: less radical measures are generally more effective and *much* easier. Here we consider your PC's processor, motherboard and memory.

BOOSTING PERFORMANCE

Upgrading the processor – or not

Imagine this manual was double its current size. Now double it again. Now cram it full of hieroglyphic tables, small print, warnings, disclaimers and impenetrable jargon. You *still* wouldn't have enough information on hand to perform a processor upgrade in all possible circumstances. There are just too many angles, too many possibilities, too many permutations to cover all bases. This book is much too short to make such an attempt. So is life. But surely, you protest, it's merely a matter of out with the old and in with the new? How hard can it be? Well, the physical procedure for changing the component is indeed straightforward, as we shall see, but *getting* to that point is fraught with difficulties. The first really seriously limiting factor is whether a new processor will even fit onto your existing motherboard.

Die used to make Pentium 4 chips.

The most common connectors

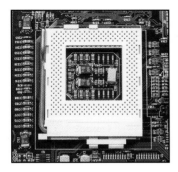

Socket 7 – *a flat socket on the motherboard. Compatible processors include: Pentium and Pentium MMX; AMD K6; Cyrix 6x86 MX and MII.*

Slot 1 – *a groove in which the processor cartridge sits on edge. Compatible processors include: Intel Celeron, Pentium II and Pentium III.*

Socket 370 – *a new style socket. Compatible processors include: Intel Celeron and Pentium III (yes, these two ranges are available in both slot and socket designs).*

Slot A – *similar to Slot 1 but designed exclusively for AMD's Athlon and Duron ranges.*

Socket A *(also known as Socket 462) – an alternative socket approach for AMD Athlon and Duron processors. There are in fact several other designs but the point holds true throughout: only a processor designed for a particular socket or slot can be used in an upgrade.*

TECHIE CORNER

The good news is that most post-Pentium processors are perfectly fast enough to cope with most computer work, short of running intensive multimedia applications and playing the latest games. If it's graphical performance you need, consider installing a new graphics card instead (p.76). The benefits will be far greater than those to be had by swapping the processor alone. Likewise, a PC's overall performance can be better improved by increasing the amount of RAM on tap (p.44), because this gives it more working space.

Remember all that 'Apollo missions were run on a calculator' stuff from the opening pages? It's time for a reality check. Do you really need a processor running at a billion clock cycles per second? No, you don't. Or if your computer usage is so intensive and demanding that you really *do* need a super-super-superfast processor at the helm, then you also need a brand new state-of-the-art system crammed with the latest complementary devices to support it. In other words, forget about an upgrade.

More things to worry about

The slot/socket compatibility issue is only one consideration.
Others include:

Front side bus (sometimes called the "system bus") speed, the
rate at which data is handled by the memory and motherboard.
This determines the true speed of a PC. The microprocessor locks
itself to a multiple of this speed. A setting called the multiplier
determines the ratio between the Front Side Bus and
microprocessor speed. If you want to up the microprocessor
speed, you'll usually have to change this multiplier. This may be a
hardware or BIOS setting (check your motherboard manual) – see
Techie Corner on p.39.

Cooling Faster processors require more cooling, either in the form
of a heatsink (a finned metal contraption that dissipates heat
through convection), or a fan, or both. Do without and it'll all go
up in smoke. Literally.

The BIOS chip (see p.145) on the motherboard may not
recognize the new processor, in which case it also needs an
upgrade. If you want the PC to restart, and we imagine that you
do, this must be done before you start work on the processor.

Does your motherboard support the required voltage of the
processor? As a rule, modern processors run at lower voltages
(i.e. cooler) than their predecessors, and a microprocessor can
quickly self-destruct if it gets the wrong voltage. It's vital to check

A motherboard bus.

BIOS (Basic Input/Output System)
is a chip on the motherboard that
controls the fundamental
operations of a computer.

that your motherboard and processor upgrade are compatible.

Consider replacing the entire motherboard replete with a new processor. It's more expensive but takes care of most worries in a single move.

Is there any point jazzing up just one component if everything else remains in place? A fast processor in an old system will run like a Ferrari in a parking lot. Have we put you off yet?

Speed demon For all their power, processors deal exclusively in the 1s and 0s of binary code. That in itself sounds baffling until you consider that a 1 is merely a signal generated by an electric current, and a 0 the lack of such a signal. The code 101, for instance, translates as power on-off-on again. The processor then runs these signals through its many, many microscopic transistors, interprets them according to certain logical rules, and outputs a binary response. Simple, huh? It's all controlled by an internal clock (of sorts) that beats at a certain rate. A 500MHz processor ticks 500 million (yes, *million*) times every single second, with each tick representing an opportunity for the processor to do something useful. Thus a 500MHz processor can do more work in a shorter time than a 200MHz model.

It's not *all* about speed, but even a cursory glance at processor technology takes you deep into a world that you really don't want to visit. Instead, here's a ready reckoner of how quickly Intel Pentium processors have evolved.

TECHIE CORNER

ZIF stands for Zero Insertion Force. Rather than having to forcibly pry a processor out of its socket with clumsy, nervous fingers, a lever unlocks it so you can simply lift the chip out. Older PCs often have a LIF (the L's for Low) socket instead, in which case there's no lever and you need a special tool called a chip remover to gently pry the processor free. Be careful when putting a processor into a low-insertion-force socket – the force required is not all that low and is perilously close to that required to crack the motherboard. Intel recommends against home replacement of LIF chips, good advice we endorse.

System Bus We mentioned the importance of system bus above. Now here's how it works. A motherboard will work with a processor that runs at a speed equivalent to the system bus speed multiplied by a factor of 0.5 and increments thereof. That is, a 60MHz bus is compatible with a 90MHz processor as in our example (60 × 1.5 = 90) or a 150MHz processor (60 × 2.5 = 150). It is not, however, compatible with a 200MHz processor, simply because 200 is not a multiple of 60.
Only the earliest Pentiums and 180MHz Pentium Pros ran with a system bus of 60MHz. 66MHz is far more common, with 100 and 133MHz now the new(ish) standards. AMD claims a bus speed of 200MHz.

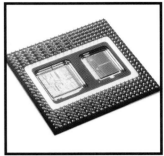

Pentium
1993
60–200MHz

Pentium Pro
1995
150–200MHz

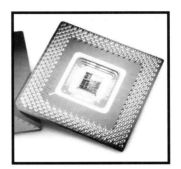

Pentium MMX
1997
166–233MHz

Pentium II
1997
233–450MHz

Pentium III
1999
450–1.13GHz

Pentium 4
2000
1.3–1.7 GHz (2Ghz in 2002)

Step-by-step processor upgrade

Still game for a processor upgrade given all the preceding observations? Fair enough. Here we perform an uncomplicated operation: replacing a Pentium 90MHz with a faster Pentium 150MHz on a ZIF Socket 7 motherboard. In this case, both processors support a system bus speed of 60MHz, and they operate at the same voltage (3.3V). One final note: always buy a retail, or boxed, version when shopping for a processor, as this will come with all the documentation you need *and* have an adequate cooling mechanism included. OEM (original equipment manufacturer: a company that buys components in bulk and builds complete systems) processors are also available and cheaper, but you'll have to source your own cooling system. That's one headache to avoid.

Before *attempting any internal work on your PC, re-read the safety precautions on p.33.*

Ensure *that you have clear access to the existing processor. This might mean temporarily unbolting the power supply unit and removing it from the case.*

Carefully *remove the existing heatsink/fan unit, usually by releasing the metal tabs at the side. Now unplug it from the motherboard and remove. Make a careful note of the location of the power connector.*

4 **Lift** *the ZIF lever to the vertical position. This frees the processor from its connector. Now it may be removed. Cartridge chips, such as the Athlon, Pentium II and some Pentium IIIs, simply unlatch and and slide from their slots.*

5 **Gently** *place the new processor on the socket. One corner should be notched (or clearly marked) to correspond with the socket so it will only fit one way. All microprocessors are coded for proper insertion. Cartridge chips are keyed to their slots. Newer socket-mount chips such as the Celeron, Pentium III and Pentium 4, are keyed by the arrangement of their pins.*

6 **Lower** *the lever to secure the processor in the socket. Latch each end of cartridge-style chips in place.*

7 **Fit** *the new heatsink/fan and connect it to the motherboard. With cartridge-style chips, it may be easier to fit the heatsink before sliding the chip into its slot.*

8 **It's time** *to think about the motherboard's system bus multiplier. We know that the system bus is 60MHz (because the manual told us so) and we know that the multiplier must currently be set to 1.5 (because the Techie Corner box on p.39 tells us so). What we must do now is make the multiplier 2.5, and this is done by adjusting the jumpers (miniature switches) on the motherboard. You see how important that motherboard manual is? In some cases, the multiplier may be set in the BIOS, which avoids such fiddling. Now put everything back together again, restart the computer, and enjoy the improved performance. It's worthwhile running your processor speed utility again (p.23) to check that the system has correctly recognized the new component.*

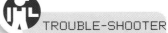

TROUBLE-SHOOTER

Really, there's nothing much that can go wrong so long as:
The new processor is fully compatible with the motherboard (system bus, speed, voltage).
It's properly and adequately cooled.
It's correctly installed in the socket.
The BIOS is capable of understanding and making sense of what's just happened.
Here are some good web resources for further reading:

http://www.pcguide.com/proc/physinst/cpu.htm

http://www.amd.com/products/cpg/athlon/howtobuild/socket_proc_install_guide.html

http://www.intel.com/overdrive/index.htm

Upgrading the motherboard – or not

Talk about putting the cart before the horse! If you can replace a motherboard, you can do just about anything (with a PC, that is). But we're not going to show you how. Why? Because every other area of this manual touches upon the motherboard in one way or another. Remember, the motherboard is the central component in a PC to which everything else is attached. Removing it to install a replacement presupposes that you know all about expansion cards, drives, channels, ports and so forth, *and* that you want to completely change the nature of your computer. Installing a new motherboard is tantamount to building a PC from scratch and is beyond the scope of this manual. However...

Mouse and *keyboard* sockets.

USB two USB interfaces for connecting external devices.

Parallel port one parallel interface, usually reserved for the printer.

Serial port one or two serial interfaces for connecting external devices (hidden below parallel port).

Three good reasons to upgrade your motherboard

You want a faster computer It's possible to buy a motherboard with a processor already installed, which means that you don't have to fuss with BIOS upgrades, voltage concerns, system bus speeds and all the rest of that malarkey.

Your old motherboard has given up the ghost It's not a common failure, but it happens. If your PC is acting up, and you're sure it's due to the motherboard – remember, this can cause a number of problems, not all of them fatal – then the PC equivalent of open-heart surgery can save the day. Why not take the chance to upgrade to a better model at the same time?

You'd like to upgrade once and once only Some modern motherboards fully incorporate all the circuitry required for graphics and sound output, and sometimes even include a modem. This makes for an economical, relatively fuss-free route to a full multimedia system.

Three good reasons *not* to upgrade your motherboard

You may have to reformat your hard disk or at least reinstall Windows. In most cases, Windows will readily adapt to a new motherboard, installing the proper drivers as required. Sometimes, however, the change may be too great and Windows will crash when it tries to cope. Reinstalling Windows should bring it to life, but you should be prepared for the additional bother.

Your old components may no longer fit. Will that old ISA soundcard find a home on your swanky new motherboard? What will you do with your PCI graphics card if the new motherboard has an AGP slot (see p.74). And what about RAM? Chances are you'll have to chuck out all your old memory and buy it fresh to comply with the new standards. If you discover that you have to buy new components throughout, wouldn't it be as cheap (and much easier) to start all over again with a new PC, perhaps hanging onto your old monitor, printer, keyboard and mouse to save a little cash? Hint: yes.

The motherboard itself may not fit. Computer cases are designed to accommodate motherboards of varying dimensions so it's never safe to assume that any old motherboard will feel at home in your PC. And what happens if the layout on the new motherboard is different and the case's power supply completely blocks access to the processor slot? You won't get very far with a brain-dead PC.

Slot 1 this is the slot version of a processor connector, as opposed to the socket design in our project example.

Memory this is where RAM is installed. In this case, we're looking at DIMM sockets.

CMOS battery a replaceable battery that keeps the CMOS alive when the power is switched off, home of all your hardware settings, see p.145.

IDE controllers the hard disk plugs into one of these and the CD-ROM drive to the other, see p.50.

Floppy disk controller yes, the floppy disk drive plugs in here.

AGP slot an expansion slot reserved for a high performance graphics card.

BIOS a memory chip that kick-starts a PC before Windows wakes up, see p.145.

Expansion slots a wide variety of expansion cards can be installed in these slots to add to a PC's features. We'll look at the different types in detail on p.74.

PART **2**

Upgrading RAM

Your PC's operating system requires a good deal of RAM (Random Access Memory) to run smoothly. Windows 95 needs at least 8MB to work at all, 16MB to work properly, and double that again to work smoothly. Windows 98 demands at least 16MB to get out of bed, but 64MB is a realistic minimum. Windows ME runs only slowly in 32MB, does better in 64MB, but really requires 128MB to keep away your yawns. Windows 2000 works well with 64MB but is also much happier with 128MB.

DDR RAM

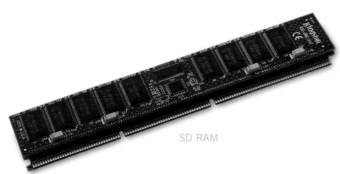

SD RAM

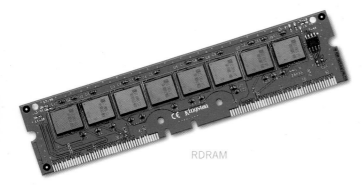

RDRAM

That's where to start with Windows XP, but most people find the new operating system happier with 256MB. Bear in mind that this is before you do anything else, anything *useful*, with your PC like write a letter or send an email. Every program you fire up operates in RAM, and every document, picture or file resides there too for as long as it's "open".

When the available memory begins to run out, as it invariably does, the first thing you notice is a general slow down in operations. Come the point of RAM overload, the PC has four choices: give up the ghost and crash; freeze unhelpfully; refuse to do another thing until you close down some programs; or magically pull some more RAM out of thin air. Thankfully, the last option is first to be followed. Windows reserves an area of the hard disk for use as a kind of pretend, or virtual, memory (and calls it a swap file). This keeps things ticking but it's woefully inefficient compared to using real RAM. If you hear your hard disk whirring and clicking a lot as you work, this is a sign of "thrashing" – i.e. the disk struggling to keep up with the pressure as Windows constantly swaps data between it and RAM in an effort to keep on top of its duties. Despite the name, it's not painful but it does nothing for performance.

All of which leads us to one inescapable conclusion: RAM is good, and more is better. What's more, it's also very straightforward to install extra memory.

What you need to know

Inevitably, RAM comes in assorted flavors and you have to be sure to buy the right type for your particular PC. Here's a guide to the critical specifications.

Capacity RAM is measured in megabytes and available in several sizes, in powers-of-two increments – 4, 8, 16, 32, 64, 128, 256 and 512MB. Old systems use small ones; today 64MB modules are most popular and affordable. We looked at how to establish how much RAM you already have onboard back on p.22.

Type Like everything else in the PC world, RAM has evolved. Brand new systems might come with souped up versions called RD or DDR RAM (Rambus Dynamic and Double Data Rate, as if you care), but your existing system will probably have EDO (Extended Data Out) or SD (Synchronous Dynamic) RAM installed. It's time to check your motherboard manual, or dig out

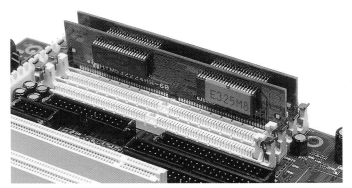

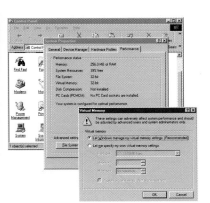

the order/delivery paperwork just to make sure. Parity can also be a concern. Most of today's PCs use non-parity memory; older systems may use parity memory; business servers use ECC (error correction code) memory. Parity memory works in non-parity systems but not vice versa. The best strategy is to match what your manual calls for.

Connector RAM comes on modules loaded with storage cells and slots into sockets on the motherboard. There are two main types: SIMM (Single Inline Memory Module) and DIMM (Dual Inline Memory Module). To fit a RAM upgrade, you either use a free slot or, if necessary, discard an existing RAM module for a higher capacity version, e.g. remove a measly 8MB module to free up space for a 64MB module.

One complication, and an important one: SIMMs *must* be grouped together in pairs, or 'banks', where each module has the same capacity. The motherboard in a typical older Pentium PC would have four sockets (i.e. two banks), so possible configurations would include:

1st bank	2 x 16MB SIMMs
2nd bank	2 x 16MB SIMMs
Total RAM	64MB
or	
1st bank	2 x 16MB SIMMs
2nd bank	2 x 32MB SIMMs
Total RAM	96MB

What you *can't* do is pluck one 16MB SIMM from its home and replace it with a 32MB module unless you simultaneously do the same with its partner. DIMMs have no such restriction. Notebooks computer usually use SoDIMMs (Small-outline DIMMs) which are DIMM shrunk down in size. As with big DIMMs, one SoDIMM makes a complete bank. Rambus comes in RIMMs, slightly larger than DIMMs, but following the same rules.

Speed It may seem odd to think of memory in terms of speed, but RAM modules talk to the processor at different rates, commonly 66, 100 and 133MHz. This is important because it relates to the speed of the chipset on the motherboard, so again check the manual and make sure you buy the fastest RAM that the motherboard supports.

PART 2

Step-by-step RAM upgrade

Here we install a new 64Mb SD RAM module in a free DIMM socket.

Before *attempting any internal work on your PC, re-read the safety precautions on p.33.*

Ensure *that you have clear access to the RAM sockets. This might mean temporarily removing other components.*

The DIMM socket *has a locking tab at either end. Press these down to the open position – i.e. angled away from the socket.*

 TECHIE CORNER

SIMMs, DIMMs and RIMMs too
How do you tell a DIMM from a SIMM? Simple: both have notches roughly in the center on their connecting edges but only a DIMM has an extra off-center notch to ensure that you can't plug it into the motherboard the wrong way around. Note that DIMMS always

install vertically (i.e. perpendicular to the motherboard) but SIMMs usually install at an angle. Instead of locking tabs, SIMM sockets generally have retaining clips at either end. Finally, DIMMs are bigger, and have 168 rather than 72 connecting pins along their base.

So what's a RIMM? Simpler still: it's a proprietary superfast design with 184 connecting pins developed by a company called Rambus, licensed to other manufacturers and only found on the very latest Pentium 4 systems.

SIMM   DIMM   RIMM

4

Line up the notches on the connecting edge of the DIMM with the socket and insert it, keeping the module vertical. Note the off-center notch that dictates which way around the module fits. If necessary, use a gentle end-to-end rocking motion to seat it in the socket.

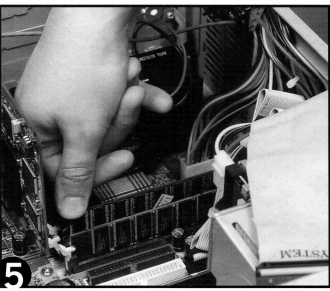

5

Push the locking tabs home to secure the DIMM. If they won't lock, press down gently on the DIMM to push it fully home.

When you restart the computer, watch the screen carefully. When the system runs through its standard memory test, just check that the total RAM reported is now 64MB greater than it was. Many PCs will say System Configuration Updated (or some such message) and may require you to press a key in acknowledgement. And that's it: no fuss with drivers, no fiddling with the configuration, just a much improved PC. Enjoy.

All you'll ever want to know about memory can be found here:
http://www.kingston.com/tools/umg/default.asp
Specific memory questions are answered here:
http://support.crucial.com/scripts/crucial.exe/faq

TROUBLE-SHOOTER

If the RAM upgrade does not register when you start the system, check the details in the General tab of the Device Manager (see p.22). If this looks right, reboot and try again.
Still not registering? Repeat the installation process and ensure that the new module is properly locked in place.
If this is a SIMM upgrade, check that you've followed the bank rules, i.e. installed two SIMMs of equal capacity in each bank.
As a final test, remove the new module and move one of the existing modules (DIMM only) into the now-vacant socket. Restart and ensure that the original

quantity RAM still registers. This way, you'll confirm that a) you're doing everything correctly; b) the socket itself is fine; c) the new module must be faulty. Exchange it!

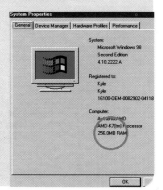

PART 3

Adding a new drive

A word about channels   50
Why upgrade your hard disk?   52
Upgrading your CD-ROM drive   58
Adding a DVD drive   64
Floppy drive replacement   68
External drives   70

Breathing new life into an ailing PC with major surgery is one thing, but there's more than one way to skin a cat (or mix a metaphor). Some of these upgrades will boost its performance, others will prolong its useful lifespan, but all will make your PC a more productive tool and/or a better toy.

A word about channels

When it comes to installing a new hard disk or, indeed, any other kind of internal drive like a CD-ROM or DVD, the first consideration is how to connect it to the rest of the computer system. What it needs is an interface of some kind, and this is where the notion of channels comes in.

A channel is a gateway that enables the exchange of data between the drive and the rest of the PC through the motherboard. The connection point itself – basically a smart plug socket – is called a host adapter. There are (of course) two possibilities.

IDE (Integrated Drive Electronics)

The most common interface for hard disk and CD drives, IDE hides under various nicknames (see Techie Corner). Virtually all motherboards have one or two IDE connectors (good for two or four drives) onboard, depending upon their age. We'll assume that you have two. In most cases, the hard disk will be connected to one controller and the CD-ROM drive to the other, both by means of flat, wide ribbon-like cables. If you examine each ribbon, you may or may not find a spare connector somewhere along its length. This is because each IDE channel can host two separate drives, one of which is designated the *master* and the other the *slave*, allowing up to four drives in a system (two masters, two

IDE adapters should be clearly marked on the motherboard. If not, they're easy enough to find.

slaves). The master–slave distinction allows your PC to distinguish between the two drives on one cable. There's no forced servitude between them – Windows merely gives the master the first available drive letter (C: in a typical system), then the next letter for the slave (or next master, if there's no slave on the channel). Otherwise the two drives are equal.

If a ribbon in your PC does *not* have a spare connector, you'll need to replace it before installing an extra drive. Often, but not always, a spare ribbon is included in the box with a new drive; otherwise, get yourself an IDE cable equipped with three connectors. You'll find two kinds: a 40-wire cable for old drives (up to 33MHz) and an 80-wire cable that's required by 66 and 100MHz drives but can be used for any IDE connection.

The advantages of going down the IDE route are pretty compelling: your PC already has the requisite circuitry in place, and the vast majority of drives come ready equipped to plug in and play with a minimum of fuss. However...

SCSI (Small Computer System Interface, but just call it 'scuzzy')

SCSI is an alternative channel with one big benefit over IDE, namely that multiple devices can share a single adapter. So, instead of a maximum of four devices sharing two IDE channels, a SCSI-equipped PC can have 7 or 15 devices all daisy-chained together – or even more if it has a second SCSI adapter. What's more, SCSI drives can be faster than their IDE counterparts. Other devices besides disks use SCSI (for example, tape drives and scanners). Moreover, SCSI allows for external connections.

But there are disadvantages. One is simply the cost: Gigabyte for gigabyte, SCSI devices are more expensive to buy. The other is that motherboards do not generally come with a SCSI host adapter onboard, which means that you have to fit one yourself before installing a SCSI device. This is as simple as fitting an expansion card (about which much more shortly) but it does use up a free expansion slot and adds considerably to the cost (and hassle).

Besides which, the difference in speed between a SCSI and an IDE drive is negligible in normal use, and it's really only servers that benefit from multiple device support. We'll assume here that IDE is your chosen course.

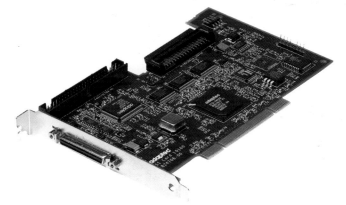

A SCSI adapter expansion card adds a new dimension to your drive possibilities but it's far from essential in a domestic computer.

TECHIE CORNER

IDE standards Just one IDE standard? That'll be the day! Here's a summary of the main specifications in the order in which they appeared. Forget what they mean, how they evolved and why they matter. All IDE drives plug into any IDE adapter. The farther down the list, however, the faster and more feature-laden the drive – but the slowest IDE device (which includes your PC's host adapter) sets the highest speed of the connection. Plug an Ultra 100 drive into an Ultra 33 adapter, and you won't get anything more than an Ultra 33 connection. Consequently, you may need a new host adapter to gain Ultra speed, and you'll definitely need an 80-wire cable for Ultra 66 speed and above.

IDE	ATA-1
EIDE	ATA-2 or Fast ATA-2
EIDE Ultra33	ATA-4, ATA/33 or UDMA/33
EIDE Ultra66	ATA-5, ATA/66 or UDMA/66
EIDE Ultra100	ATA-6, ATA/100 or UDMA/100
ATAPI	an IDE standard that supports drives that aren't hard disks like CD-ROM and DVD.

PART 3

Why upgrade your hard disk?

Here's a funny thing: no matter why you first bought your PC, you're almost certainly using it for something entirely different now. As we become more proficient and confident, we explore new avenues and discover just what all this hardware and software can really do for us. Thus it's no surprise to find a book-keeping machine roped into editing digital video or a system purchased primarily for internet access functioning as a full-blown home entertainment center. That's why upgrading a PC is so often a compelling, and frequently pressing, affair.

One of the key components that comes under pressure soonest is the hard disk. It's amazing just how quickly a seemingly cavernous disk can fill to capacity. A single megabyte might be sufficient storage space for the entire text of a novel, but that equates to a mere six seconds or so of uncompressed music. Throw in a few high resolution images or video files and take into account the size of modern software applications, including the operating system itself, and it's little wonder that we run out of space sooner than we thought possible. This is when our thoughts turn to upgrading the hard disk.

When your hard disk falls behind the times, it's time to upgrade.

External hard disks are portable, practical – and pricey.

Zip drives are ideal for backing up 100 or 250MB of data at a time.

For mass storage, nothing beats a tape drive.

How to upgrade...

There are essentially three upgrade options. First, you might install a secondary hard disk alongside your existing one, akin to building a warehouse in the car park. Alternatively, you might prefer to *replace* your existing hard disk. This has the virtue of neatness but the distinct disadvantages that you must also reinstall the operating system from scratch and somehow transfer all your existing files onto the new disk. Of course, if your original disk was to suddenly fail – a rare occurrence but always a possibility – this might be your only option.

Finally, you might decide on an external hard disk. Such a solution costs more to buy, and gets even more expensive if you have to buy a special controller card on top. If it connects to the PC through a slower external parallel or USB interface, it will be much slower at saving data too. Then again, a FireWire or external SCSI drive can offer higher speeds than a plain old IDE drive. What's more, you can take the entire shebang with you wherever you wander and quickly plug it into any other PC. What better way to carry 20GB of data in your pocket?

...and how not to

If storage space is your only concern, do consider some form of removable media. For instance, a recordable CD drive could be used to permanently archive all your older files and thus lighten the load on the hard disk. A high-end Zip drive is another possibility (250MB per disk), as are Jaz (2GB per disk) and tape drives (10 or 15GB for starters).

Windows also provides a few good simple tools that can make a big difference to a hard disk's performance *and* free up considerable space. Don't spend a penny before reading Part 6.

Iomega's Jaz drive holds a massive 2GB per cartridge.

What you need to know

The hard disk is a device used for storing data. Unlike RAM, where data is held in a kind of dynamic flux, files once saved to the hard disk are housed in safe storage. These files can, of course, be retrieved from the hard disk and altered, deleted or simply re-saved at will, but they don't disappear when the power is switched off. The hard disk *drive* is the mechanism that spins the actual disk, and moves the magnetic heads that do the hard work as well as the case in which it's all held. But since the disk and the drive are in practice inseparable, we'll call the whole assembly a hard *disk*.

As well as choosing between an IDE or SCSI interface and coming to grips with the EIDE/ATA/DMA muddle, certain other specifications should be considered before you go shopping.

Capacity Without question, size matters when it comes to hard disks. Modern disks can top 60GB and we'd certainly suggest that 10GB is the absolute minimum for a secondary disk.

Speed #1 Not an obvious consideration, perhaps, but hard disks spin at different rates. You'll see rotational speeds of 5,400, 7,200 and 10,000rpm, and it doesn't hurt to get the nimblest disk that you can afford because the faster the disk spins, the faster it can spit out data to your eagerly waiting computer. Note, however, that it's never worth upgrading a hard disk for speed alone. We're talking about differences on the scale of milliseconds.

Mounting brackets enable a 3.5 inch drive to use a 5.25 inch bay.

See Appendix 2 for a word about BIOS and CMOS.

Speed #2 Drives are also rated by interface speed – the Ultra 33, 66 or 100. This is the number of megahertz at which the drive *could possibly* transfer data. Newer drives have higher potentials, but with reasonable drives you need not worry. With drives smaller than 40GB and 7200rpm or slower, you'll see little difference between 33MHz and higher speeds. Moreover, your host adapter must have the same high-speed potential. You won't see the benefits of an Ultra 66 (or UDMA-66) drive if you only have a UDMA-33 controller. In general, just plug in and don't worry about it. But if you plan eventually to move your new drive to a faster computer, look for a quicker drive.

Drive size Internal hard disks are 3.5-inch drives. This is fine so long as you have a free 3.5-inch drive bay available – most do, but you'll probably have to open up the case to find out for sure. If you have to put your 3.5-inch drive in a 5.25-inch bay, you'll need a mounting adapter. Many drives include them, or you can get one where you buy your drive.

Setup software New hard disks must be formatted before they work, and some come with their own setup software that makes this a breeze. Most setup software now allows you to duplicate your old drive – programs and data – on your new drive, so you can quickly subsitute the new drive for old (and even boot from it). Check – and go for the easy option every time!

A word of warning

If your motherboard is more than a few years old, there may be three distinct problems with its BIOS. On one hand, it may not recognize disks larger than 504MB, in which case your new toy is going to be invisible to the PC. On the other hand, if the BIOS is a little younger but still no spring chicken, it may not recognize disks larger than 2, 3 or 8GB – in which case ditto. However, many drives come with slick software that can circumvent these issues, or you could always upgrade the BIOS first. Note that if your motherboard has EIDE controllers onboard (as opposed to plain IDE), no problem: your BIOS is just fine.

But on the third and final hand, only a 'plug and play' BIOS chip will automatically recognize a new hard disk and supply CMOS (see Appendix 2 on p.145) with all the information it needs (specifically, how many cylinders, heads and sectors the disk has). Failing that, you'll have to manually enter all this stuff in CMOS yourself. Although this isn't actually too difficult, it can seem a daunting, non-intuitive procedure for a novice and we wouldn't recommend it unless you're absolutely confident of getting it right. Our advice would be to consider an internal hard disk upgrade only if you are sure your BIOS supports large drives and recognizes them automatically. Realistically speaking, if you cannot upgrade your BIOS to handle a big new hard disk, it's probably too old and slow for a hard disk upgrade anyway.

PART 3

Step-by-step hard disk upgrade

Before *attempting any internal work on your PC, re-read the safety precautions on p.33.*

Make sure *that you can access the drive bay. Sometimes this means removing a plastic cover on the front of the case. Also check how to secure it in place. Usually this is a simple case of inserting screws on either side of the bay, but occasionally a sliding rail mechanism is used for 5.25-inch drives. Position the disk in its bay.*

A secondary *hard disk should be installed on the same IDE channel as the primary disk, which means that it should use the same ribbon cable. So, follow the ribbon cable from the existing disk all the way back to the motherboard and check that there's a spare connector.*

While *you're here, double-check that there's a spare power lead within reach. This is a four-wire cable with a white connector (identical to those already supplying power to the primary disk and CD-ROM drive). If there's no spare lead, purchase a Y-shaped 'splitter' that turns one connector into two.*

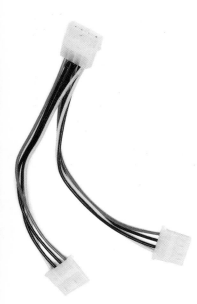

A splitter overcomes a shortage of power cables.

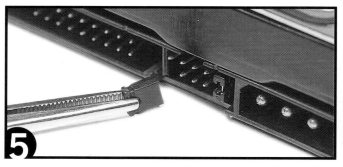

Having *ascertained that you can fit and secure the disk, remove it and look around the back. Here you will find a number of metal pins and a plastic 'shunt' or two. These are jumpers, used to determine whether this is going to be the master or the slave device on this IDE channel. The primary hard disk – i.e. the disk that contains Windows – is always the master. Therefore, as we are installing a secondary hard disk for storage purposes only, it's the slave. Check the settings of both drives on the channel – sometimes you have to adjust your existing drive, too, if it has been configured to be the only drive on the channel. Check the manual that came with the disk for instructions on how to set the jumpers appropriately.*

Now *reinsert the drive, attach the ribbon cable and power leads gently but firmly, and secure the disk in place. If you're screwing it in place, make sure you use short screws (no more than one-quarter-inch long) and don't over-tighten the screws as they mustn't poke too deeply into the bowels of the drive. Take a deep breath, put it all back together again, and restart the computer.*

What happens next?

This depends upon whether you have a plug and play BIOS chip on your motherboard. If so, lucky you: the computer now knows that a disk has been added and all you have to do is partition and format the new drive ready for use. If *not*, you'll have to manually enter details about the disk in CMOS (see Appendix 2), and you're most certainly going to need the documentation that came with the hard disk.

This may seem like an awful palaver. That's because it is an awful palaver. Here comes another one…

Partitioning and formatting your new hard disk

We'll look at the merits of sub-dividing a hard disk into manageable chunks (see Appendix 3) but for now simply note that you have to first partition and then format your new component before you can do anything with it. This is when its own specialist setup software or a third party utility can make life much easier. However, we'll assume here that you have neither.

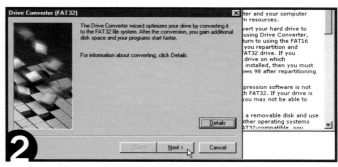

Click Start *point to Run, and then type command. At a command prompt, type fdisk, and then press ENTER. As the program starts, it will ask if you want to enable large disk support. With a new drive, you will always want to do this, so type "Y". (You won't get this question if you have Windows 95. Win95 OSR2 first added this support to fdisk.) The fdisk program will continue loading then display the above menu.*
Press 5 *and then press ENTER. When you do this, the selection changes from the physical disk 1 (master) to the physical disk 2 (slave).*
Press 2 *and press ENTER.*
Press 1 *to select the Create DOS partition or Logical DOS Drive menu option, press ENTER,*

Press 2 *to select the Create Extended DOS Partition menu option, and then press ENTER. Restart your computer to start Windows.*

NB: *For more in-depth instructions on partitioning and formatting, Microsoft provides an excellent article in its Knowledge Base on the web. You can find it at:*
http://support.microsoft.com/support/kb/articles/q255/8/67.asp

PART  Upgrading your CD-ROM drive

There are three reasons why you might consider upgrading your CD-ROM drive (apart from hardware failure, of course): to install software more quickly; to play CD-based games more smoothly; or to add extra features.

Like everything else, CD-ROM standards have evolved and today's drives are very much faster than yesterday's. Naturally enough, a fast drive can transfer data into the main computer system more quickly than a slow drive, so you'll see a big difference when you install a program on the scale of, say, an office suite. But just how often do you do that? Will the few minutes you save justify the time and expense of upgrading? Probably not.

CD speed rarely limits the performance of 3D action games. While a faster drive certainly can't hurt, a good games machine will benefit far more from a turbocharged graphics card and superfast processor than a mere CD-ROM upgrade.

No, the only really good reason to rip out a functioning CD-ROM drive is to add to your computer's powers. That's exactly what we'll look at here: adding a *recordable* CD drive.

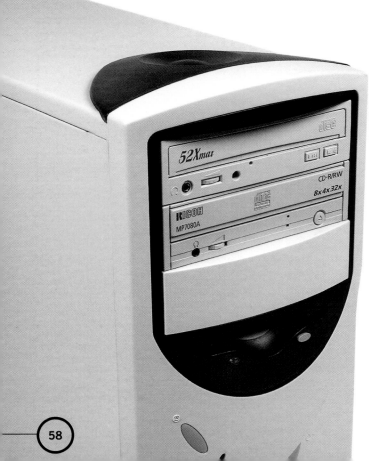

A recordable CD drive gives you better backup options – and makes audio CDs to boot.

Drive Information

Please select a CD-R/CD-RW drive to continue

My Computer
E:\
Backup1 (G:)

DirectCD Disc Ready

The disc is ready for read/write access directly through drive (G:). You may start reading and writing the disc using Windows Explorer, or any other Windows application such as Microsoft Word.

Display this notification again when a DirectCD disc is ready for read and write.

OK

Packet writing software lets you fill a CD in bits and pieces rather than all at once.

Recordable drives

A CD-ROM drive can read data stored on standard CD-ROM discs such as those used to distribute software programs. It can also read audio CDs and relay the signal to a sound card in order for your PC to play music. What it expressly can *not* do is record data onto a disc. For that, you need either a CD-Recordable (CD-R) or a CD-Rewriteable (CD-RW) drive. The difference is simply this: CD-R drives use discs that cannot be erased and reused, whereas CD-RW drives use discs that can be re-recorded many times over. In fact, a CD-RW drive also works with CD-R discs, making it by far the better buy now that there is no appreciable price difference between the two technologies. We'll assume this to be the case.

A single recordable disc holds at least 650MB of data – that's a massive 450 times more stuff than fits on a floppy disk – so the potential for archiving old files and making critical backups should be clear. Furthermore, with the right software it's easy to record your own audio compilations that can be played on household stereo equipment (note that some older car stereos won't play CD-R audio CDs) or make direct copies of existing CDs – as long as you don't infringe copyright.

Drive	Media	Pros	Cons
CD-ROM (read-only memory)	Reads any standard CD-ROM, CD-R or audio disc. Will also read "finished" CD-RW discs	Essential equipment in any PC onto disc	Cannot record (save) files
CD-R (recordable)	As above but also records on blank CD-R discs. These discs can be filled in a series of distinct sessions or piecemeal using packet writing software	Ideal for backing up and archiving data, copying discs and making audio compilations	Once full, a CD-R disc can not be re-recorded
CD-RW (rewriteable)	As above but records on both blank CD-R and CD-RW discs	Maximum flexibility as you can use CD-R or CD-RW discs to suit the task in hand	Audio CD-RW discs are not always playable on domestic stereo equipment. Older CD-ROM drives can also struggle with CD-RW discs)

CD-Rs can be written to multiple times until they are full. However, each extra "session" you add to the disc has an overhead of 13MB so it's not ideal for adding lots of little files all the time. But thanks to the minor miracle of "packet writing" software, now you can treat a CD-R or CD-RW disc just like a giant floppy and fill it up piece by piece, file by file. You might, for instance, make a daily backup of your critical work documents.

Add or replace? It's perfectly possible to install a CD-RW drive (or CD-R – the process is identical) alongside an existing CD-ROM drive but there's little or no point. For one thing, your new recordable drive also functions as a CD-ROM drive, and is likely to be a good deal faster than the old one. For another, replacing the drive means that you save both an IDE channel (more on this in a moment) and a drive bay (ditto). Also, to play audio discs, including multimedia presentations like encyclopedias, the drive must connect to the sound card. Some cards only support one device which effectively renders one or other of the drives mute. Besides all of which, it's just as easy, if not easier, to make a direct swap – and isn't that what it's all about?

The one exception would be if you're planning to regularly make copies of CDs. In this case, it's worth keeping the old drive for direct CD-to-CD copying, as otherwise the data has to be extracted from the original disc and written to the hard disk before a recording can commence.

TECHIE CORNER

Optical media Broadly speaking, two methods of data storage are used in a computer system: *magnetic* media, as in the hard and floppy disks; and *optical* media, as in a compact disc (recordable or otherwise). Optical in this context means that a laser reads light patterns reflected by the disc. In a recordable drive, the laser writes data to the disc by "burning" pits in a malleable layer. This is quite a different process to that used in industry, where compact discs are pressed rather than burned, but the effect is much the same. Incidentally, as a rule (and a perfectly silly one at that) the term *disc* is generally used when referring to optical media like CDs and *disk* when referring to magnetic media. That's the convention we're following here. For more on CD technology, start here: **http://www.cdrfaq.org/ http://www.pctechguide.com/ 08cd-rom.htm http://www.pcguide.com/ref/cd**

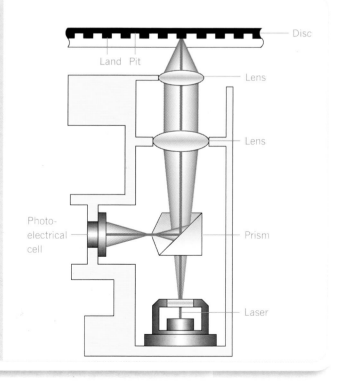

What you need to know

Praise be, recordable CD specs are nowhere near as complicated as you might expect. The critical considerations are these:

Speed A drive's speed is primarily a measure of how quickly the disc spins and therefore how quickly data is read and passed to the main system. It's a *little* more complicated than that – there's all that business about variable and constant velocities, seek times and access times – but let's not worry about it. The first generation of CD-ROM drives transferred data at a rate of 150 Kilobytes per second, referred to hereafter as 1x speed. Later models spin the discs faster – 2x, 4x, 8x, 12x, 16x, 24x, 32x and so on – with corresponding improvements in performance. However, 16x is generally regarded as quite fast enough for practical purposes so don't get hung up on drives claiming ludicrous and largely pointless 100x speeds.

Note that a CD-RW has three separate speed ratings: read, record (or write) and rewrite describing the drive's performance as a CD-R, CD-RW and CD-ROM (in that order), such as 12x/8x/32x. A CD-R drive only has read and record (write) speeds.

Media As discussed above, different drives work with different types of discs. CD-RW is the most flexible because it can read CD-ROM and audio discs and record on both recordable (cheap) and rewriteable (not so cheap) discs. However, CD-R discs offer greater compatibility and are thus better suited to audio compilations, transferring files from one PC to another and sharing data with others. Size-wise, blank discs generally have a capacity of 650MB (equivalent to 74 minutes of music) or 700MB (80 minutes) and are priced accordingly.

Blank recordable discs are now affordable and reliable. Choose CD-R for maximum compatibility.

PART 3 Step-by-step CD-RW drive upgrade

Before *attempting any internal work on your PC, re-read the safety precautions on p.33.*

The existing *CD-ROM drive is wired up to a power supply, a ribbon cable connected to an IDE controller on the motherboard and an audio cable connected to the sound card. Unplug the cables from the drive (not the motherboard!) but keep the connectors within reach. You'll need them again in a moment.*

The drive *is secured in the bay with four short screws, two on either side. Remove these and set aside, and slide the drive forward until it's free.*

...and more of what you need to know

CD-R discs are also speed rated. You must match the media to the writing speed that you will use, such as 12x.

Interface Like the hard disk, an internal CD drive connects to the rest of the computer through a channel (see p.50), usually the secondary IDE channel (although any modern IDE connection works). Some CD drives have SCSI connections. These have their own benefits, but installing one invariably means installing a SCSI controller expansion card first (although some old sound cards actually had a SCSI adapter built in for just this purpose). We'll go down the more common IDE route here.

Drive bay CD drives of all persuasions use the standard 5.25 "half height" inch drive bay (see p-19). Assuming that your PC already has a CD-ROM drive installed, there will almost certainly be at least one free drive bay either above or below it. You may have to pry or snap off a plastic cover to gain access. In this example, of course, we're going to use the old drive's bay for the new device.

Alternatively, you could buy an *external* recordable CD drive for added convenience and portability. Parallel drives are painfully slow, USB less so, and FireWire almost as speedy as internal devices (although, again, you'll almost certainly have to install a FireWire expansion card first).

Don't play with your PC while burning a CD if you want to avoid buffer under-run.

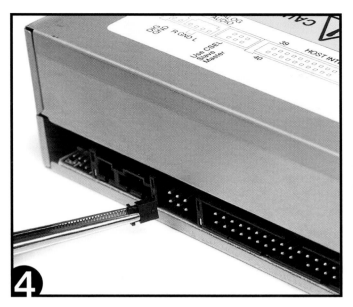

4

5

6

Before installing the new drive, check the jumper settings. If the drive is to be installed by itself on the secondary IDE channel, as is the norm whith a single CD device, these should be set to master. However, if the drive is to share a channel with the hard disk (i.e. connected to the same ribbon cable), the hard disk should be designated master and the CD drive slave. (If two drives on the same channel were both set to master or slave, neither would work). Check the documentation that came with the drive if it's not clear how to set the jumpers.

Now slide the new drive into the vacant drive bay, secure with the screws you removed earlier and connect the power, ribbon and audio cable exactly as they were connected to the original drive. Carefully put everything back together, take that familiar deep breath, and switch on.

Your new drive should now work immediately but now is the time to install and experiment with the application software that came with the drive, as without it you can't start recording.

Buffer stuff If a PC fails to supply data to the drive quickly enough during a recording process, the drive temporarily runs out of work. It cannot hold its place on the rapidly spinning disc while waiting for more data, and it cannot go back. The result is what PC people call a 'coaster', an unusable CD that is suited only for protecting antique coffee tables from cold drinks. The technical name for the problem is buffer under-run and it's a mighty pain in the posterior. To help alleviate it, drives come with built-in buffers. Look for at least 2 or 4MB. Better still, the latest generation of recordable drives carry a 'burnproof' tag (the 'burn' bit stems confusingly from buffer under-run) which means that a drive can start recording precisely where it left off in the case of interruption. Get one if you can.

TROUBLE-SHOOTER

If your new drive refuses to play an audio CD – and your old one worked just fine – check that the audio cable is correctly connected. It's a little plug that can easily be missed.

Any new recordable CD drive will come with *some* recording software but typically only the minimum required for rudimentary data backups. To record audio CDs or fill CDs with data piecemeal (packet writing), you may have to purchase a specialized program or two. Roxio (**http://www.roxio.com**) and

Ahead Software (**http://www.nero.com**) are leading manufacturers.

If repeated buffer under-run threatens your sanity and you have more coasters than cups, choose a lower writing speed – for example, 2x instead of 8x. (Some CD-R makers suggest defragmenting your hard disk, too.) This usually solves the problem. Some older drives and software don't take well to multi-tasking. Doing anything else at the same time as writing a disc increases the likelihood of under-run.

PART  Adding a DVD drive

The first D stands for Digital, the second for Disc, and the V for Video, Versatile or nothing in particular, depending who you ask. Officially, it's versatile but most DVDs store videos, at least today. They look just like any old CDs but with one big difference: vastly increased capacity, anywhere from 4.7GB to 17GB, to be precise – and, yes, that means that a single disc quite possibly holds more data than your current hard disk. The popularity of DVD is mainly due to the fact that a single disc can store and play a full-length feature film at a remarkably high quality level. Some weighty software programs, particularly reference titles crammed with film and sound clips, are also distributed on DVD.

What's more, a DVD-ROM drive (ROM as in read-only memory i.e. no recording ability) can also play CD-ROM, CD-R and CD-RW discs. Some very clever 'combo' DVD drives even combine the recording functionality of a CD-RW drive with DVD playback. In the name of making life as simple as possible, our ever-present mantra, such a drive is the best upgrade of all. Why fuss with separate CD-ROM, CD-RW and DVD drives when a single device does the lot?

Large software programs are sometimes distributed in DVD format for convenience.

A DVD drive turns your PC into a home cinema.

Don't forget to install a software
player if you want to watch
movies on your computer.

What you need to know

There are several critical considerations before you splash out
on DVD.

Speed DVD drives are rated in terms of how quickly they spin,
just like CD drives, but a 4x DVD and 4x CD move data at vastly
different speeds. For every 'x' a DVD drive is about six times
faster than a CD drive.

Interface Internal DVD drives use either the IDE or, more rarely,
SCSI interface. Installing one is almost as straightforward as
fitting a recordable CD drive. However…

Hardware acceleration Playing DVD movies on a computer
demands a great deal in the way of system resources, and only a
mid-range Pentium II processor or better is up to the task. This is
because the video on a disc is considerably compressed and must
be decompressed by the computer during playback. If the
processor lags behind, the result is a jerky picture or outright
failure. But all is not lost as it's possible to install a dedicated DVD
decoder expansion card to take the burden away from the system
processor, with the result that even humble Pentium systems can
play jitter-free films. The decoder card uses a PCI slot on the
motherboard (see p.74) and thus involves a little more surgery
than fitting a drive alone. It's also a more expensive option than
buying a standalone drive. Then again, you get the benefit of
Dolby Digital sound (see p.81) directly from the decoder card.

Graphics Getting high quality video demands a comparatively
recent graphics card – specifically, one that supports MPEG-2
video – although any good quality monitor will suffice. However,
if you're fitting a decoder card at the same time, you should find
a 'system video' output which enables you to connect a television
set instead of a monitor. Ideal for family viewing.

Sound A good sound card is also a must as older models will not
necessarily support the high quality digital audio output used in
DVD films.

Software You'll also need to install playback software to watch
a movie on your monitor but something suitable may come in
the box with the drive. If not, there are plenty of programs to
choose from.

DIY DVD But what, you cry, about recordable DVD? Well, it's
possible but as we write this particular field is awash with
incompatible and competing standards and it's anybody's guess
which one will come out on top. There's DVD-R, DVD-RAM,
DVD-RW, DVD+RW… we could go on. However, not one of
these standards enables you to burn a *movie* onto disc, and they
can't record audio CDs either. Recordable DVD is thus really only
a compelling consideration if you have vast quantities of data to
archive, and even then we'd suggest waiting until the current
confusion resolves itself.

PART  Step-by-step DVD drive upgrade

The process is essentially the same as installing a recordable CD drive (see p.62). You might choose to replace the existing CD-ROM drive or you might already have installed a CD-RW drive and now want a DVD drive to complete your system.

In the latter case, the procedure is still identical except that the new device requires a free 5.25 inch drive bay and it will certainly have to share an IDE channel with another device. If possible, connect the DVD drive to the same channel as the CD-RW drive rather than the hard disk. Set the jumpers on the DVD drive to slave if you share a channel (for example, with your CD-RW drive), or to master if the DVD is the only device on the channel.

As discussed above, you'll have to install a separate decoder card if you're installing the drive in a pre-Pentium II system. We cover the general procedure for fitting expansion cards on p.78 but there is also some fiddling with cables in the present example, as the decoder card must hook up to both the sound card and the monitor. The DVD drive's manual will explain what to do but essentially there are two steps:

A DVD decoder card is essential for jitter-free playback in older systems.

TECHIE CORNER

Regional coding
It's a drag but DVD movies are cobbled with "regional coding", a copyright protection measure which means that discs designed for distribution in one region do not play in drives built for other regions. In other words, only buy a disc that matches the coding of your drive. The current regions are as follows:

Code	Region
1	USA & Canada
2	Europe & Japan
3	South East Asia
4	Latin America & Australia
5	Russia, Africa and rest of Asia
6	China

Either *connect the supplied audio cable between the decoder card and the DVD drive and run a second cable between the decoder card and the sound card internally; or connect the supplied audio cable between the decoder card and the DVD drive as in the previous step but reassemble the case with the decoder and sound cards unconnected. Then run a patch cable (a short cable supplied with the drive) between the external 'audio out' connector on the sound card (unplug the speakers) to the external 'audio in' connector on the decoder card. Finally, plug the speakers into the 'audio out' connector on the decoder card.*

Disconnect *the monitor cable from the graphics card and run the supplied patch cable between the "video out" connector on the graphics card to the decoder card's "video in" connector. Now plug the monitor cable into the decoder card. (Note: Some decoders instead require an internal link – check your manual.)*

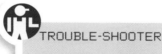TROUBLE-SHOOTER

As with installing a new CD drive, you are unlikely to run into hardware problems so long as both the BIOS (see p.145) and device are plug and play and you connect all the cables correctly.

By far the most common complaint is poor quality playback when watching a DVD movie, and this is almost always because the computer's resources are overstretched. Even with a decoder card on board, you really don't want to be writing a novel, surfing the web, sending email and checking your accounts while a movie is playing, so close down all other programs for the duration of the

show.

DVD playback software can also be problematic. In particular, not all programs support all audio formats. To learn more about this still emerging technology,

try these sites:
**http://www.pctechguide.com/
10dvd.htm
http://www.intervideo.com
http://www.3dsl.com**

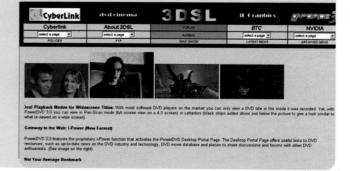

Step-by-step floppy drive replacement

Ah, the good old floppy drive. Slow as a sloth and capable of storing a paltry 1.44MB of data per disk, it's still a staple component in virtually every PC. The drive isn't something that you'll *upgrade* as such – there's only one standard and it's not getting any better or faster – but just occasionally a drive may give up the ghost and need replacing. You may be tempted not to bother, figuring that you use the thing so rarely that it's not worth the bother, but a quick re-read of p.26 should help change your mind. Should Windows start acting strange, the first place you'll turn to is your startup disk – which, without a working drive to read it, is about as useful as a glass baseball bat.

Before attempting any internal work on your PC, re-read the safety precautions on p.33.

Actually, there's one circumstance in which an upgrade is called for, and that's if your PC has a 'single-sided' drive onboard. Such a drive uses 720KB floppy disks and you don't see many of them around these days. It's an unlikely scenario in a modern-ish machine but just thought we'd mention it.

What you need to know

In truth, there's little we need to say about the floppy drive other than that it uses a 3.5 inch drive bay, has its very own dedicated channel on the motherboard, and costs next to nothing these days. So let's skip straight to an installation.

The much-maligned floppy drive is still an essential in most computer systems.

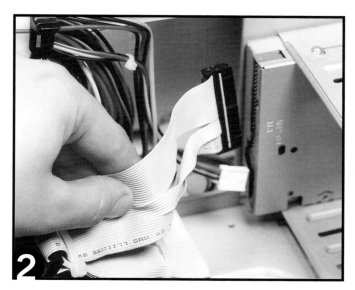

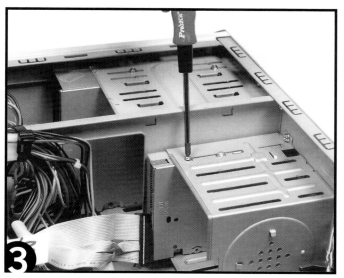

The existing *floppy drive is wired up to a power supply and a ribbon cable (connected to the floppy drive controller on the motherboard, usually close to but always distinct from the IDE controllers). Note the peculiar split and twist in the cable. This dictates which device is designated as drive letter A:. Unplug the cables from the drive (not the motherboard) but keep the connectors within easy reach. You'll need them all again in a moment. Note that the power connector is usually smaller than the one used to wire up the CD drive.*

The drive *is secured in the bay with four short screws, two on either side. Remove these and set aside, and slide the drive forward until it's free. Occasionally, a 3.5-inch drive may be installed in a 5.25-inch bay, in which case you'll need an adapter (which you can buy where you get the drive). Make sure you can replicate the procedure with your new device.*

TECHIE CORNER

One alternative you might consider is an LS-120 SuperDisk drive: basically, an improved, proprietary version of the floppy drive that uses 120MB disks *and* reads standard floppies into the bargain. However, this device must be installed on an IDE channel just like a hard disk or a CD drive, which limits further your expansion possibilities. There can also be problems getting BIOS to recognize the drive as bootable. For full product details, see: **http://www.imation.com.**

Slide *the drive in position in its bay and connect the power and ribbon cables exactly as they were connected to the original drive.*

Put *everything back together again, restart the system, pop a floppy disk in the drive and make sure that Windows can read from it. You might also like to reboot with your startup disk (see p.26) in the drive just to be certain that the drive works properly in an emergency.*

PART 3

External drives

We've looked in detail at hard disks, CD and floppy drives, and pretty much any internal drive can be installed in exactly the same way. A tape drive for commercial backups is one popular option; a Zip or Jaz drive for low-cost, flexible, removable storage is another. The limiting factor is really the IDE controllers on the motherboard. Four devices – including the hard disk but excluding the floppy drive – are usually as far as you can go without resorting to high-tech trickery or installing an additional host adapter. Only the most recent PCs extend support to a four channels/eight drive configuration.

Pros and cons

However, in every case it's just as possible to opt for an *external* drive. True, these are always a little more expensive as you pay for a protective case, a power supply, a button or two and perhaps a panel of blinking lights (for which read: external drives are something of a rip-off), but the advantages are considerable:

An external drive is portable, which means you can use it at home and in the office *and* hook it up to just about any PC anywhere. This is especially true of the latest 'hot-swappable' USB and FireWire devices which are operational almost as soon as you plug them in.

Because they simply plug into a port around the back of your PC, or perhaps into a USB hub incorporated within the monitor housing or built into the keyboard, external drives are easier to install (not that installing an internal drive is any great drama, as we hope to have demonstrated).

It's always easier to find what's wrong with a device when you can see it (and give it a shake), especially if it has self-diagnostics measures built in. And it's *much* easier to take back to the shop if it's a DOA dud.

As for the disadvantages… well, external drives need their own power source (or, sometimes, batteries), they take up room on a desk, they may have to share a port with other external devices, they're slower than their internal counterparts, and they demand that price premium we mentioned. Oh, and they're more prone to coffee spills.

External drives offer unlimited upgrade options without the need for surgery. What's more, you can take the devices from PC to PC and use them anywhere.

PART  # Expansion cards

A word about architecture **74**
Upgrading your graphics card **76**
Upgrading your sound card **80**
Upgrading your modem **84**
Adding USB **87**

After decades of hardware evolution, today's PC has emerged with a plethora of different standards and interfaces, counter-intuitive design standards and an acronym soup of a language to make "sense" of it all. But not to worry: upgrading an expansion card remains one of the most effective ways to revamp a crusty old computer. It's easy when you know how – so let's go find out.

PART **4** A word about architecture

Today's motherboards combine historical standards with the latest and fastest interfaces.

As we have seen, the motherboard is the central component in your PC system, so much so that everything else connects to it one way or another. An interface is simply a gateway through which any two components or devices can "talk" to each other. We've looked already at how internal drives use the IDE interface, talked about slots and sockets for processors, and plugged extra memory straight into the motherboard. Now let's turn to expansion cards.

Get slotted

Expansion slots are connectors on a motherboard used for attaching printed circuit boards (cards). The beauty of such a system is that you can immeasurably improve the performance of your computer without wielding a soldering iron. There are three main expansion slot standards (in order of age):

ISA (Industry Standard Architecture). ISA slots are black, long, slow and all but obsolete. You're most likely to find a modem in one. Or dust. Expect to find a couple inside the case in all but the most recent PCs.

PCI (Peripheral Component Interconnect). The PCI standard is faster than ISA and its slots (white, short) typically host sound cards, older graphics cards and perhaps a DVD decoder. A USB or SCSI host adapter can also be bolted on through the PCI interface to give a computer still more interface options. Three slots is an acceptable minimum, four is better, and more are always welcome.

AGP (Accelerated Graphics Port). This is a slot designed exclusively for modern graphics cards, specifically optimized for 3-dimensional effects and digital video. There is only ever one AGP slot per motherboard, and you'll only find it on Pentium II systems and above. However, a modern machine is no cast-iron guarantee of AGP as some motherboards incorporate the necessary graphics chips directly within the motherboard itself.

Blank check

Expansion slots are positioned on the motherboard in such a way that one end of an installed card pokes through the PC's rear panel. Flick back to p.17 and note how the graphics connector (a plug for the monitor) and the audio connector (a plug for speakers) are accessible externally. Or just peek around the back of your computer to see the visible end of your installed cards. The holes that afford expansion cards access to the outside world are usually covered with metal blanking plates but these can be easily removed.

One factor to watch: it's not uncommon for adjacent PCI and ISA slots to share a blanking plate, with the implication that you can install one or the other type of card but not both simultaneously. Newer motherboards may also have an AMR (Audio Modem Riser) or CNR (Communications and Networking Riser) slot which also encroaches on the array of blanking plates.

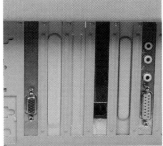

Blanking plates can be removed to open up access to expansion slots.

Integration

Back on p.15, we mentioned that some motherboards incorporate a variety of features within their own circuitry, specifically graphical and sound output and sometimes a modem or network card. The alleged attractions of such an approach are price (it's cheaper to build and buy a PC with an "integrated" motherboard than one bustling with expansion cards) and ease of use (because there's no need for the hapless PC owner to open the lid and poke around inside). Some of these totally integrated systems let you switch off the motherboard sound or video and install standard sound boards or graphics adapter in their expansion slots. Some, however, are so integrated they lack expansion slots. Certainly, we are not inclined to recommend a non-expandable system unless you're quite sure that you won't want to upgrade your computer a year or two down the line (it's a bold buyer who would make such a claim) or you're buying a basic office-based system as opposed to a funky, multifunctional, all-singing, all-dancing affair for the home.

Let's now look in some detail at three popular and worthwhile expansion card upgrades.

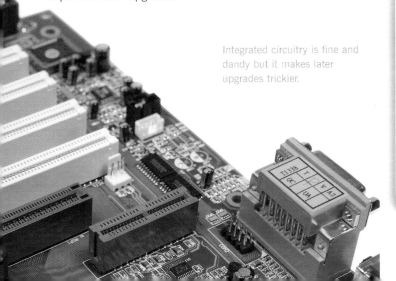

Integrated circuitry is fine and dandy but it makes later upgrades trickier.

TECHIE CORNER

Bits and buses The physical path between any two computer components – in other words, the wires that make the connection – is called a bus. The size, or width, of the bus is a measure of how much data it can handle at any one time. The ISA standard is based on a 16-bit bus, which means that it transfers a maximum of 16 bits of data per processor cycle (a bit being the smallest binary unit i.e. a single 1 or 0). PCI is a 32-bit standard and is thus capable of twice the workload within the same time. When we say that one interface is "faster" than another,

this is simply shorthand for saying that it's capable of sustaining a higher rate of data transfer. Although AGP is also 32-bits wide, it operates at twice the speed of PCI (66MHz rather than 33MHz) and is thus better suited to the high demands of graphics cards where a great deal of data has to be processed as quickly as possible to keep video and games in full flow. Newer PCs have 2x or 4x AGP ports, which operate at the faster rates the numbers imply. For (much) more on AGP, look here: **http://developer.intel.com/ technology/agp**

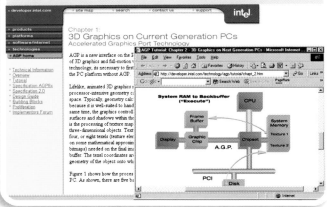

PART **4** Upgrading your graphics card

Perhaps you want to edit digital video footage on your PC. Maybe you'd like to add a TV tuner card and use it as a television. If you've developed an interest in photography, your old graphics card may be unable to display your digital snapshots in all their glory. In all these cases and more, a graphics card upgrade is likely to be a good investment.

But one word of caution: if you intend to turn your PC into a games machine then yes, you'll need a state of the art graphics card – but you'll *also* need a fast processor, bags of RAM, a reasonable sound card, probably a joystick, a decent monitor and stacks of free hard disk space. For just having fun, a standalone games console may be a better bet. Indeed, a console *plus* a new portable television can cost less than the hardware upgrades you'll need to transform a basic PC.

That said, the popularity of computer games has been directly responsible for some remarkable technological advances, and you will certainly be impressed with the performance of the latest graphics hardware if your experience of gaming begins and ends with Solitaire. The best strategy is to choose the platform – PC or game machine – for which you can get the most games that you want to play.

Solitaire won't strain your graphics card but digital video might.

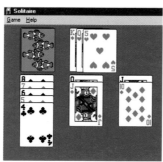

Resolving resolution Your PC's graphics card and monitor are inextricably entwined. The monitor displays the picture but the picture itself is generated by the graphics card (also called the video card or board). For best results, you want the card and the monitor working together to mutual advantage.

Consider the question of resolution: a measure of how much detail you see on screen. A resolution of 800 x 600 (a standard known as SVGA, or Super Video Graphics Array) means that an image is composed of 600 rows of 800 pixels (tiny points of light). A higher resolution like 1280 x 1024 equates to many more pixels, and that in turn means that more images can be squeezed onto the screen without loss of detail. The images do, however, get smaller.

Now, graphics cards usually support many different resolutions but there is a physical limit on any given monitor's maximum display. What it boils down to is this: if you have a 15 inch monitor and don't plan to replace it any time soon, a basic graphics card that supports a resolution of 800 x 600 is all you really need. By contrast, low resolution is wasted on a 21 inch monster monitor; you'll be far more satisfied with a 1600 x 1200 display.

Flat panel monitors based on the same LCD technology used by notebook computers are rapidly becoming affordable. At a given size, an LCD screen shows you more detail than a conventional monitor. Consequently, most 15-inch flat panels offer 1024 x 768 resolution. Be careful when you buy. Only flat panels with analog (or VGA) inputs plug into conventional graphics cards. Flat panels with digital video inputs (DVI) require special graphics adapters.

Here are the recommended optimum display settings

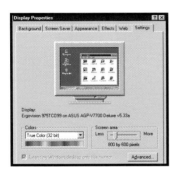

Screen size *15 inch*
Resolution ***800 x 600***

*Screen size **17 inch***
*Resolution **1024 x 768***

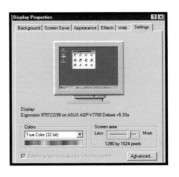

*Screen size **19 inch***
*Resolution **1280 x 1024***

*Screen size **21 inch***
*Resolution **1600 x 1200***

What you need to know

Graphics cards are plagued with technical specifications and you need to understand at least the basics in order to make an informed purchase.

Interface As discussed earlier, graphics cards use either a PCI or an AGP slot. The big advantage of AGP is that the card can access main system RAM quickly, which avoids bottlenecks and boosts performance. It would be very unusual to find an AGP-equipped motherboard with a PCI graphics card installed, but in such circumstances you would certainly want to upgrade to AGP. Curiously, for reasons that we'll come to in the monitor section, you might want to leave an old PCI card in place while upgrading to AGP; similarly, adding a PCI card alongside an AGP card would count as an upgrade (we're talking about running a dual monitor setup, in case you can't contain your excitement). But in most cases you'll swap one AGP or PCI card for another of the same type.

Memory Graphics cards come with their own slice of memory onboard. How much dictates just what it can do, and how quickly. For 3-D gaming, look for 64Mb or more (and be prepared to pay top dollar).

Memory also determines how many colors the card can display. If you right-click on the Windows Desktop, select Properties and click on the Settings tab, you'll see your current card's color setting. If you now try to increase the setting – say, from 256 to 65,000 (16-bit) – you may find that the resolution slider automatically adjusts to a lower setting. This is because cards can typically pump out a full color range at a low resolution *or* a high resolution in fewer colors, but not both simultaneously.

Memory matters, particularly in gaming. The minimum a modern graphics board offers, typically 4MB, will get you to 1280 x 1024 resolution in TrueColor (24 bits) for business work, but the 3D circuitry on game boards goes through memory like heirs through an estate. You'll want 64MB or more for today's games.

Today's graphics cards use the AGP slot and come with their own memory chips.

PART **4**

Step-by-step graphics card upgrade

The beauty of expansion slot architecture is that internal cards can be installed and uninstalled with virtually no effort. Here we replace an AGP graphics card with another.

Before attempting any internal work on your PC, re-read the safety precautions on p33. Be sure to ground yourself and wear your antistatic wrist-strap, as expansion cards are very susceptible to static charges. Keep your new card in its antistatic bag until the last moment.

A single screw secures the graphics card to the chassis. Remove this now and set aside.

Carefully remove the old graphics card from its slot. You may find retaining clips that must be removed. Hold the card by the edges and be sure not to damage its components with your fingers. This can be a tricky business, particularly if there are other expansion cards either side, and it might take a little effort to get the card free. Do not rock it from side to side.

TROUBLE-SHOOTER

Never upgrade a graphics card and a monitor simultaneously. From a diagnostic point of view, you only want to work with one suspect device at a time. If Windows will only start in Safe Mode, the card's refresh rate is probably set too high for the monitor. Lower the setting in Display Properties. Click Start, Control Panel and Display, and look in the Adapter tab. Your monitor probably has its own display settings, usually accessible through buttons on its casing, and you may wish to adjust the brightness or contrast to optimize the display. You can also adjust the image size to suit the viewable screen area.

...and more of what you need to know

Processor Yes, graphics cards also have processors. As you would expect, the faster the processor, the better the card is at rendering complex graphics. Look for the term 'graphics accelerator' or, for the ultimate hardware high, a GPU (Graphics Processing Unit). Cooling fans are now commonplace.

Dimensions In ye olden days, graphics cards were two dimensional affairs, perfectly adequate for office-style work but hopeless for playing games or displaying digital video. Then along came 3-D graphics cards that sat in a slot alongside the existing 2-D model and kicked in when intensive video rendering was called for. This was clearly a ridiculous set of affairs and so, in time, evolved the next generation of cards that combined 2- and 3-D functions. Badly. Some time thereafter, *good* combo cards emerged, and that's where we are today. Incidentally, 3-D isn't really three dimensional; it's just clever trickery that adds the illusion of depth to video presentations.

External connectors Before buying any new graphics card, consider carefully just what you want it to do. If its sole responsibility is to work with your PC monitor, no problem: any card will do that. But if you want to watch games or DVD movies on a TV screen, an S-Video output would be useful. Some cards are equipped with video in connectors so you can capture video from a camcorder or VHS recorder, and you might even find a connector for 3-D glasses (be prepared to be ridiculed by your family and friends).

Take *the new card from its antistatic bag and gently insert it in the vacant AGP slot, making sure to match its connecting edge precisely with the slot opening. Again, be sure not to touch the card's components. If necessary, use a gentle end-to-end rocking motion to ease it into the slot.*

Now *secure the card to the chassis using the screw that you removed earlier. Also reattach any retaining clips, if possible.*

Carefully *put everything back together, reconnect the monitor cable, and switch on the PC. All being well, Windows will detect the new card, launch the New Hardware Found wizard and prompt you for the appropriate drivers. Have any CD or floppy disks that came with the drive at hand along with your Windows installation disc and follow the instructions. Alternatively, you may have to manually install the driver by running a setup program from the supplied disk. It's impossible to be definitive here as procedures vary, but the manual should make clear what to do.*

As well *as a driver to get the PC and the monitor talking to each other, your new graphics card may well come with additional software tools and toys, including games demos, a DVD player, utilities for adjusting display settings, an electronic manual and goodness knows what else. We'd suggest installing everything to start with and removing any bits and pieces you don't want.*

 TECHIE CORNER

Display settings Changing the display settings *before* upgrading your graphics card can help to avert problems with Windows. If the new card's manual says something along the lines of: "change your display driver to Standard VGA," proceed as follows (note: the precise wording may vary)

1 Click Start, point to Settings, click Control Panel, and then double-click Display.
2 Click the Settings tab, and then click Advanced.
3 Click the Adapter tab, and then click Change.
4 Click Next, click "Display a list of all the drivers in a specific location so you can select the driver you want," then click Next.
5 Click Show All Devices.
6 In the Manufacturers box, click (Standard Display Types).
7 In the Models box, click Standard Display Adapter (VGA), click OK, and then click Next.

8 Click Next, click Next, and then click Finish.
9 Click Close, click Close again, and then click Yes to restart your computer.

NB: The above instructions are adapted from Microsoft's Knowledge Base on the web and used with permission. For more information, look here:
http://support.microsoft.com/ support/kb/articles/Q127/1/39.ASP
An alternative approach is to uninstall the original card's drivers through the Add/Remove Programs utility (see p.120) just before switching off the PC and installing the new card.

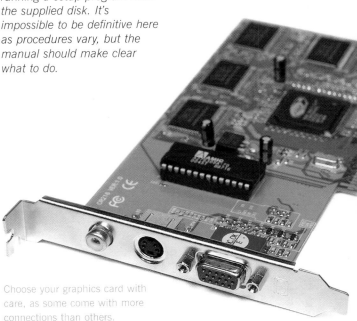

Choose your graphics card with care, as some come with more connections than others.

PART 4 Upgrading your sound card

Time was when the average desktop PC emitted only feeble and occasional bleeps. But these days even the humblest domestic computer is a veritable home entertainment center. A sound card is standard equipment in any new system, as are, unfortunately, cheap, tinny speakers that do it no justice whatsoever. More on them later but for now merely note that good speakers can enhance sound quality up to a point but the sound itself is generated internally. A powerful sound card is the starting point for aural satisfaction.

With a decent sound card onboard, your PC can eclipse your stereo in the audio stakes.

Why bother? Do you really want your PC to double as a stereo? Well, yes if you want to play audio CDs on your computer. Thanks to the phenomenal popularity of the MP3 file format and the widespread distribution (and piracy) of music on the internet, you could even build and play a music collection entirely on and from your hard disk. And then there are multimedia presentations like encyclopedias and reference titles. And DVD movie soundtracks. And computer games. And sound files on web pages. And internet-based radio and TV channels. And so on...

Moreover, a sound card means that you can record your *own* music on your computer if you have the mind and/or the talent to do such a thing. Have you considered the benefits of internet telephony where long-distance calls on the internet cost a fraction of normal telephone charges? There's also the evolving world of voice recognition: speak into a microphone and smart software transcribes your words onto the page as text.

All of these examples require a sound card. The good news is that your PC almost certainly has one onboard already; the better news is that the quality and flexibility of sound technology has appreciated dramatically these past few years, yet even top of the range hardware is realistically priced. So, if your card is found wanting, dump it and drop in a new one.

First, of course, and as always, do a little research.

What you need to know

Figuring out which card best suits your needs is not too tricky if you keep an eye on the following considerations:

Interface Modern sound cards all use the PCI (32-bit) expansion slot. There's every possibility that your existing card is in an ISA (16-bit) slot but it's time to bid it a fond farewell – as long as you have a spare PCI slot.

3-D Three dimensional audio is basically surround sound stereo. You'll need a whole bunch of speakers for the full effect (see p.102) but there's nothing quite like it for realism. If you're serious about your sound, read and absorb these sites: http://www.dolby.com/digital http://www.3dsoundsurge.com

MIDI or Musical Instrument Digital Interface – is as the name suggests an interface that enables a musical instrument (typically a keyboard) to connect to the sound card in order to play and record music. The technology is also widely used in computer games so a MIDI-capable card is a must.

Wave table (WAV) A wave table card (see Techie Corner overleaf) is essential for audio fidelity. The quality of a card's sound is measured in terms of bits, where more is better. Go for a 64-bit card if you intend to record your own music or are prepared to invest in speakers that make the most of the card's superior output; otherwise, a 32-bit card will suffice.

Duplex means that a sound card can make and record sounds simultaneously. Most conversations are duplex to some degree – we talk and listen at the same time – so a full duplex card is essential for PC chat and telephony.

External connectors Important connectors include a speaker output (which also works for headphones), a line output (to play back through your stereo), a line input (to record from your stereo), and a microphone input. Most sound boards have only three jacks – boards meant for good-quality sound omit the speaker jack; others omit the microphone or line input. Many sound cards also come with a connector for a joystick or other type of games controller.

Modern sound cards use the more powerful PCI interface.

You can make your own music with a sound card but don't forget decent speakers.

PART **4** # Step-by-step sound card upgrade

Upgrading a sound card is just as straightforward as replacing a graphics card. In this example, we'll remove the original card from its ISA slot and install a new PCI card.

Before attempting any internal work on your PC, re-read the safety precautions on p.33. Be sure to ground yourself and wear your antistatic wrist-strap, as expansion cards are very susceptible to static charges. Keep your new card in its antistatic bag until the last moment.

Note the thin audio cable connecting the sound card to the CD-ROM (or CD-RW) drive. Carefully unplug this at the sound card end only.

A single screw secures the sound card to the chassis. Remove this now and set aside.

TECHIE CORNER

Sampling Way back yonder, sound cards used a technology called FM (Frequency Modulation) Synthesis whereby the tone of, say, a violin was generated according to complex mathematical formulae. This worked just fine as far as it went but you'd never be fooled into thinking a Grapelli was in the room. A radically different technology called wave table synthesis was then developed. Here, actual recordings – *samples* – of musical instruments are digitized, stored in memory and called upon to reproduce truly lifelike music. It's still synthetic, of course, but it's the next best thing to housing a miniaturized orchestra in your PC.

Carefully remove the old sound card from its ISA slot. Hold the card by the edges and be sure not to damage its components with your fingers. This can be a tricky business, particularly if there are other expansion cards either side, and it might take a little effort to get the card free. Do not rock it from side to side.

Take the new card from its antistatic bag and position it gently on but not in a free PCI slot. This is just to check which metal blanking plate on the chassis needs to be removed in order that the card can access the outside world.

Replace the card in its bag while you remove both the retaining screw and the blanking plate.

Gently insert the new card in the PCI slot, making sure to match its connecting edge precisely with the slot opening. Again, be sure not to touch the card's components. If necessary, use a gentle end-to-end rocking motion to ease it into the slot.

Now secure the card to the chassis using the screw that held the blanking plate in place or one that came with the drive. You may also care to close up the ISA slot's hole with the blanking plate. This will reduce interference and keep mice from nesting in your computer.

Attach the audio cable to the appropriate connector on the card (consult the manual for directions). In the unlikely event that the plug on the audio cable doesn't fit your new card's connector – a sign of changing standards – use the cable supplied in the box (assuming that there is such a thing). You will of course have to connect it to both the sound card and the CD drive. Carefully put everything back together, reconnect the speakers, and switch on the PC. All being well, Windows will detect the new card, launch the New Hardware Found wizard and prompt you for the appropriate drivers. Have any CD or floppy disks that came with the card at hand along with your Windows installation disc and follow the instructions.

TROUBLE-SHOOTER

Never upgrade a sound card and speakers simultaneously! From a diagnostic point of view, you only want to work with one suspect device at a time.

No sound when you play an audio CD? Did the speakers work just fine with the old card? Try plugging headphones into the CD-ROM drive (there should be a jack on the front) to make sure that both the drive and your CD playback software are working. If so, and if you have a suitable cable, connect the headphone socket to the audio *input* on the sound card. If you can hear the CD through the speakers now, the problem lies with the

internal audio cable. Open the PC (after taking all the usual precautions) and ensure that it's correctly connected at both ends. Replace if necessary.

Just on the off-chance, double-click the speaker icon in the System Tray (the right hand end of the Windows Taskbar) and make sure

that the CD drive has not been muted.

Also try playing audio files saved on the hard disk. If necessary, use the Windows Find Files tool to seek out files with the extension WAV.

Look in Device Manager (see p.22) and ensure that the sound card icon is not flagged with an exclamation or question mark (this would indicate a problem or conflict).

Modern sound card software is often fiendishly complex. There will likely be a host of settings to play around with, probably some diagnostic tools too, and almost certainly much less help in the manual than you would like. Look

for an electronic manual on the supplied CD-ROM or consult the card manufacturer's website for further help.

PART ④ Upgrading your modem

Modems come in all shapes and sizes but it's speed that really counts.

Modems are now a standard computer accessory. In fact, you quite possibly bought a computer in the first place precisely *because* it had a modem onboard. There may be cheaper, more convenient and in many ways better ways to get online, but the PC modem still provides the most common route into cyberspace.

If your current system does not have a modem, there are plenty of reasons to add one: to access email, the world wide web, newsgroups, bulletin boards and all the other areas of the internet; to send and receive (paperless) faxes; to set up your computer as a basic telephone answering machine or an advanced voicemail system. But there's only one good reason to *upgrade* a modem, apart from hardware failure, and that's to take advantage of the latest standards.

Ins and outs Although most new computers have modems fitted internally, we would strongly suggest that you consider purchasing an external modem this time around. Yes, they are slightly more expensive (although probably not as much as you'd expect) but they have several distinct advantages over their internal expansion card counterparts. Namely:

Diagnostics All external modems have an array of blinking lights that reveal what it's up to at any precise moment e.g. sending a fax or downloading a file from the internet. This makes it much easier to diagnose problems. Indeed, simply switching a modem off and back on again resolves many a headache. Just try doing *that* with an internal model.

Where would we be without the wonders of the world wide web?

Installation External modems use either a serial or a USB port. These are real, physical connections that leave little room for doubt. Internal modems, by contrast, use a kind of virtual port (usually called COM 3 or COM 4), and installing Windows drivers can on occasion prove troublesome.

Convenience An external modem leaves an internal expansion slot free for another device. Remember, you only have so many slots to go around.

The right software can turn your PC into a communications center.

What you need to know

A glance at the specification sheet of a standard modem would put you to sleep in an instant. We're going to ignore the intricacies of error correction, data compression, protocols and parity because it's immensely dull and irrelevant in the current context. Here instead are the essentials:

Speed Measured in bits per second (bps). An analog modem downloads data at a maximum rate of 56,000bps, which is why so many of us spend so much time waiting for web pages to load in our browsers. Old modems followed the V.90 standard, which has been replaced by V.92. The difference is that new modems connect quicker (but still transfer at the same speed). For details see **http://www.v92.com**.

If your PC has a slower 28,800 or 33,600bps modem, you should see some improvement from an upgrade to V.90 or V.92. Web pages will appear more quickly and large emails won't take quite so long to download.

Fax A fax modem copies or *emulates* the workings of a standard fax machine (which is, after all, just another device that sends analog data through the telephone line). This means that you can prepare a letter in your word processor program and fax it anywhere in the world without having to print it out and feed it through a standalone fax machine. Almost but not quite all modems can do this: look for the word fax on the box or a standard called CCITT Group 3 Fax.

Voice A voice-enabled modem works just like an answering machine – it intercepts incoming calls, plays a recorded greeting and lets callers leave messages – but with the right software you can also set up and manage a complex voicemail service. Usually, the computer must be switched on and connected to the phone line for this to work, but some *external* modems are smart enough to answer the phone and take messages all by themselves.

TECHIE CORNER

Broadband If ever a technology was in a state of flux, broadband internet access is it. Depending on where you live in the world and how much you're prepared to pay, cable or DSL (Digital Subscriber Line) connections may or may not be available. In the current market, figure either costs about twice as much as dial-up modem access (around $50 per month). These services promise download speeds more than 10 times that of a humble modem. DSL speed depends on how far you live from the telephone company central office (the closer, the faster it can be, from about 384Kbps to 1.5Mbps.) Cable can be even faster, but you share a connection so your speed may plummet evenings when the Web is popular. To make the connection, cable requires a cable modem; DSL requires a "router." Both are external devices that your supplier will provide with the installation of the service. You connect them through a standard network port. If you don't have the right port, you can install one in your PC as you would any other expansion board. The broadband dream is that one day everybody will have an always-on, affordable, fast

internet connection (remember the "information superhighway"?). But we're not there yet. Not by a long shot – as you may discover when you try to order DSL or cable service. To learn more about the different routes online, start here:
www.cablemodemhelp.com
www.adsl.com
To find out whether you can get DSL in your area, check with your telephone company or these major DSL wholesalers:
www.covad.com
www.rhythms.com

What's in a name? Modem is an acronym for modulator/demodulator. In a nutshell, a modem converts the digital language of computers into a series of beeps and whistles that can be sent down a telephone line and converted back into digital data by a modem at the other end of the line. Typically, the other modem belongs to an Internet Service Provider which then connects you to the internet at large. Hence you get to surf the web and send email through your telephone line. It's all terribly clever – but not, unfortunately, terribly swift.

Software Modems rely on application software to do their thing. All that you need to access the internet is built into Windows but "communications software" is designed specifically to handle fax and voice functions. Any new modem should come with at least a basic communications package in the box.

So, in summary, if you want a good modem look for V.92, fax and voice. And if you want an easy life, opt for an external model.

Installing your new modem The method for installing an internal modem is precisely the same as that for installing a graphics or a sound card: take all the usual precautions, plug it into a free expansion slot (either PCI or ISA, depending on the model), put everything back together again and restart your computer. At this point, the New Hardware Found wizard should appear and prompt you for the driver. Pop the supplied CD-ROM in its drive and follow the onscreen instructions.

An internal modem is neater and cheaper but an external model is portable and easier to trouble shoot

TROUBLE-SHOOTER

Uninstall the drivers for any existing internal modem *before* installing a new modem in the same expansion slot. Go to the Device Manager tab in System properties (see p.22), highlight the modem's icon, and click Remove. Now switch off the computer and install the new device. This should help ensure that Windows prompts for the new driver through the New Hardware Found wizard.

Just installed a V.90 or V.92 modem and you can't connect at 56,000bps? Join the club. 56K is a theoretical speed which is seldom (okay, never) achieved in real life. This is due to various factors, including but not limited to the volume of internet traffic, the age and quality of your telephone wiring, and the mood of the gods. Single-level standards imposed by the FCC specifically limit V.90 and V.92 speed to 53K. Connection speeds of around 40K are average and, sad to say, as good as you're likely to get without a broadband connection.

Some internal modems have two connectors on the external faceplate: one for a cable that runs to the phone socket on the wall; and one into which a telephone extension may be plugged. Failing this, you can buy a two-into-one adapter for the wall socket and so connect both the modem and a telephone. You can't use both at once, of course – a live internet connection ties up the telephone line just like a regular call – but it does save fiddling around with plugs.

Most hassles are related one way or another to Dial-Up Networking, the Windows program that a modem uses to connect to an ISP. See p.140 for help with common problems.

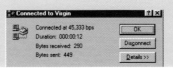

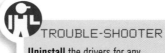

86

EXPANSION CARDS

Adding USB

We've looked at installing a graphics card, a sound card and an internal modem. However, expansion slots are such a versatile part of a PC that there are many other possibilities. One such is adding a FireWire (or IEEE 1394 card, to be precise and pedantic) card. This introduces an extremely fast interface ideally suited to capturing film footage from a digital camcorder onto your PC.

Another popular option is adding a network interface card in order to connect two or more computers together. Commonplace in the work environment, this is rapidly becoming a popular option at home where more and more of us have two serviceable PCs. Networking allows the machines to share many of the same resources, such as printers and an internet connection. We've also mentioned SCSI (Small Computer Systems Interface) several times in passing: a fast interface that lets you hook up multiple devices daisy-chain fashion. This too requires little more effort than installing a controller card in a free PCI slot. But we're going to look here at installing another type of controller: one that at a stroke transforms an older, clunky computer system into a versatile powerhouse. We're talking, of course, about USB.

Up for it? The main factor to consider is your PC's operating system. The first release of Windows 95 and everything that went before it had no support whatsoever for USB, so installing a controller card achieved precisely nothing. Windows 95b (also called OSR2) introduced limited USB support, but it was only with Windows 98 that full compatibility was guaranteed. Hence any Win95-ers out there need to upgrade your operating system or stop reading now.

There's also a question of whether or not your hardware is capable of supporting USB. Intel has a free software utility called USBready that can give your PC a complete once over for USB readiness. Download it here: **http://www.usb.org/data/usbready.exe**

SCSI is ideal for daisy-chaining multiple devices. But do you actually have multiple SCSI devices?

Check that your system can use USB before you take the plunge.

A simple USB expansion card is one of the most worthwhile upgrades for an older system.

USB is about to get its first major speed upgrade.

What you need to know

USB, or Universal Serial Bus, is a relatively modern interface for external devices with several distinct advantages over its serial and parallel predecessors.

It's quite fast By which we mean that a fair bit of data can pass through a USB bus in a short time. The existing version of USB (1.1) has a top speed of 1.5MB per second; the new version 2.0 – or Hi-Speed USB – will run at up to 60MB per second (more than twice as fast as FireWire). Hold on to your hats and keep an eye on **http://www.usb.org** for details.

It's flexible You can connect a number of USB devices (up to 127, theoretically) by installing hubs – expansion boxes with multiple USB ports – at strategic points. Many keyboards and monitors come with USB hubs built in. Note that you can't simply daisy-chain USB devices together.

It's widespread After a slow start in the PC world, the USB interface is now routinely supported on a whole range of devices, including printers, scanners, keyboards, mice, joysticks, external CD and DVD drives, tape and Zip drives, digital cameras, webcams, handheld PDA-style computers, speakers, modems and more.

It's "plug and play" This means that Windows will (or certainly should) recognize any USB device as soon as it's plugged in and prompt for the drivers immediately i.e. no rebooting. No fussing with jumpers or other tricky hardware settings either.

It's hot-swappable Instead of having to reboot your PC every time you connect a device, you can plug and unplug the likes of a USB digital camera and use it immediately.

It's a power supply too! Well, up to a point. USB provides easily enough power to run less intensive devices like webcams and modems, which certainly helps to keep the cable spaghetti to a minimum. Some higher powered devices like Zip drives and scanners can also be run directly from a USB port but not from a non-powered hub.

TECHIE CORNER

U-S-B Let's consider this acronym. "U" is for *universal*, a reflection of the fact that a single, standardized connector and cable combination works with all USB devices. That means no more fiddling with X-to-Y-to-Z-to-whatever adapters and odd-shaped, proprietary plugs. "S" is for *serial*, which means that data passes through the connection one bit at a time (as opposed to *parallel*, in which several bits go through together). And "B" is for *bus*, which is just the wiring along which data flows. So now you know.

Some monitors have powered USB hubs built-in – perfect for hooking-up additional devices.

PART  Step-by-step USB card upgrade

USB controller cards typically come with two or four USB connectors and use the PCI expansion slot. Sounds simple? It is. Here's how.

Before attempting any internal work on your PC, re-read the safety precautions on p.33. Be sure to ground yourself and wear your antistatic wrist-strap, as expansion cards are very susceptible to static charges.

Take the new card from its antistatic bag and position it gently on but not in a free PCI slot. This is just to check which metal blanking plate needs to be removed in order for the card to access the outside world.

Replace the card in its bag while you remove both the retaining screw and the blanking plate.

TROUBLE-SHOOTER

There's nothing much that can go wrong providing you install the controller card correctly. However, here are a couple of things to look out for:

USB cables have different connectors on either end. The flatter, wider connector – Type A – goes to the USB port, and the squat, square Type B connector goes to the device. *Never* use a cable with Type A connectors on both ends to try to wire two

computers together. For one thing, such cables are illegal; for another, you'll blow up both PCs and burn down your house.

Don't buy a USB cable longer than 15 feet. It won't work. If you really need to cover a long distance, either add a powered hub every 15 feet or daisy-chain together up to five 'active extension' cables to boost the signal.

Take out the new USB card again and gently insert it in the vacant PCI slot, making sure to match its connecting edge precisely with the slot opening. Be sure to hold the card carefully without touching its components. If necessary, use a gentle end-to-end rocking motion to ease it into the slot.

Now secure the card to the chassis using the screw that held the blanking plate in place. Carefully put everything back together and switch on the PC. All being well, Windows will detect the new card, launch the New Hardware Found wizard and prompt you for the appropriate drivers. Have any CD or floppy disks that came with the card at hand along with your Windows installation disc and follow the instructions.

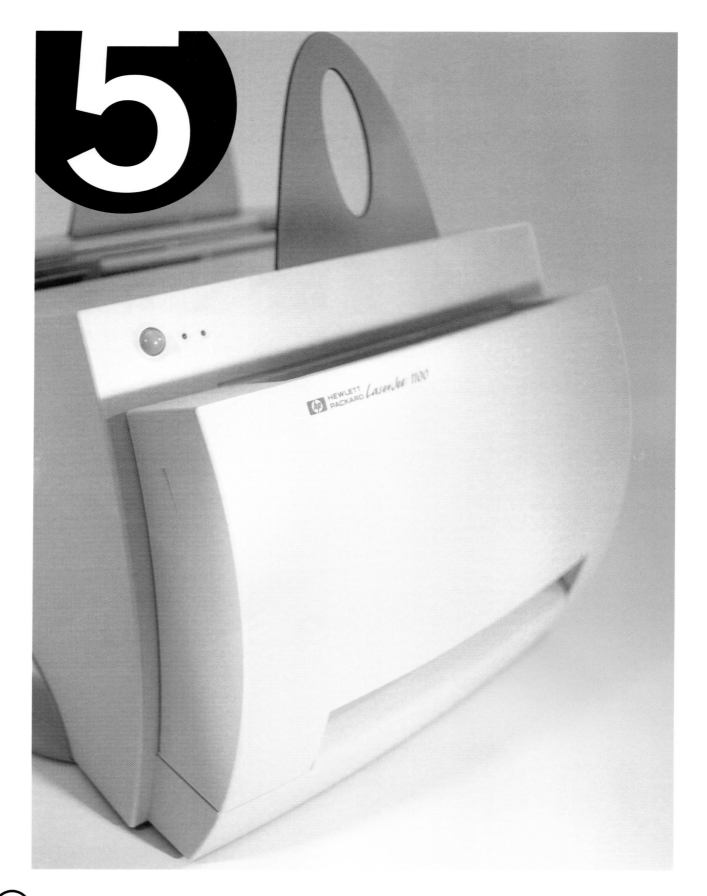

PART 5

Peripheral devices

Upgrading your monitor   92
Upgrading your keyboard   97
Upgrading your mouse   100
Upgrading your speakers   102
Upgrading your printer   104
Upgrading your scanner   110

A peripheral device is any component in a computer system that isn't actually the computer itself. If you take away the processor, memory and motherboard, all you're left with is a box of bits that falls some way short of a working PC. But the monitor, keyboard, mouse and printer are mere add-ons. So too are the hard disk, CD-ROM and floppy drive. Here we'll look at upgrading the most common external peripherals, beginning with the most important – and expensive – of them all.

PART  Upgrading your monitor

Because monitors are so pricey, manufacturers and retailers of budget – and even high-end – computer systems tend to cut corners here first. But while a 15-inch display unit looked just fine in the shop, do you now find yourself shuffling the chair ever closer each day just to see what's going on? Has the picture lost some of its sparkle and color depth? Have you taken up digital photography or computer gaming and found that your aging monitor no longer cuts the mustard? It's time to save your eyesight and go for a bigger, better model. Choose wisely and it will serve you well for years – and, unlike the rest of your system, it won't be obsolete as soon as you get it home.

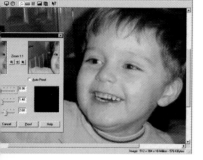

If digital photography is a hobby, you'll need a good monitor to see the results at their best.

What you need to know

There are two main types of computer monitor: CRT (Cathode Ray Tube) and LCD (Liquid Crystal Display). Here's a brief summary of the pros and cons.

Screen size The screen size of a monitor is a diagonal measurement from corner to corner. However, while a 17 inch LCD model will indeed have a viewable screen of 17 inches, as you would hope and expect, the same size of CRT monitor typically offers a *viewable* screen size of only 16 inches or less. This is because the quoted figure is a measure of the cathode ray tube itself, part of which is always hidden from view by the

monitor housing. Indeed, we've seen 17 inch monitors that offer just a fraction over 15 inches of visible screen. Look for an "actual screen area" figure, or whip out a tape measure and make your own comparisons.

Distortion Thanks to clever manufacturing techniques, CRT screens are now much flatter than they once were. This helps to reduce distortion, especially around the edges. Best of the bunch are imaginatively called "flat," as opposed to "flat squared" or "spherical" (avoid). LCD screens are perfectly flat so distortion issues don't arise.

Infact, there are several different manufacturing techniques and monitor standards. The two terms you are most likely to encounter are *shadow mask* and *aperture grill*. The first incorporates a perforated sheet of metal that focuses electron beams onto the screen, often used in FST (Flat Square Tube) models where the curvature of the glass is minimized. The second replaces the perforated sheet with a series of vertical wires through which the beams are channeled. These are held in place by one or two horizontal wires that can usually be seen (just) if you stare at the screen hard enough. Some people find this irritating but the aperture grill approach means that almost completely flat glass can be used to make a monitor. To find out more, look here: **http://www.iiyama.com/support2/tech.htm**

The distance between the holes in the shadow mask is called the dot-pitch, and it represents the smallest detail that the screen can display. (The corresponding term for aperture grills is slot-pitch.) Finer (smaller numbers) is better – look for figures near 0.25 millimeter.

Resolution We discussed resolution on p.76, where we pointed out that the graphics card and monitor should be matched to produce the best quality picture. However, CRT monitors generally run well and look good at a full range of resolutions whereas LCD screens are optimized to work at a single resolution. If you need flexibility here, particularly for playing games, CRT is the better option.

TECHIE CORNER

CRT and LCD – the difference!
Do you really want to know? Trusty old cathode ray tube technology works by firing a beam of electrons at the screen in order to stimulate red, blue and green phosphor dots. By continually drawing lines across the screen, the beam paints a picture across the entire viewable area. Then it does the same thing over and over again many times per second (the refresh rate). In an LCD monitor, a liquid crystal solution is suspended between two sheets and an electric current switches individual cells on and off to block light or let it pass through. Or, to cut a long story short, CRT works just like your television and LCD just like your digital watch. For full details, look here:
http://www.pctechguide.com/06crtmon.htm
http://www.pctechguide.com/07panels.htm

CRT Screen

- Inner magnetic shield
- Electron gun
- Electron beam
- Shadow mask
- Funnel glass
- Frame
- Panel glass
- Phosphor screen

LCD Screen

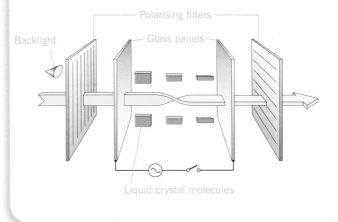

- Polarising filters
- Backlight
- Glass panels
- Liquid crystal molecules

Refresh rate A measure of how many times per second the monitor redraws the image on screen. As a rule, the higher the resolution, the harder it is to maintain a high refresh rate; as another, a high refresh rate means less visible flicker, and that means no headaches or eyestrain. Look for a CRT monitor capable of sustaining a refresh rate of 85Hz at a resolution of 1024 x 768, and at least 75Hz at 1280 x 1024. (Refresh rates are not so important with LCD monitors thanks to the different display technology: around 60Hz is acceptable.)

Dimensions No comparison here. CRT monitors are big, bulky and heavy; LCDs are neater, much shallower and relatively lightweight. If you're pushed for space or don't fancy bashing a hole in your wall to accommodate the rear end of a CRT monitor, stretch the budget and splash out on LCD. Alternatively, consider 'short neck' CRT monitors where a premium price buys a much reduced tube depth.

Viewing angle CRT screens can be viewed from just about any angle – try it and see – but you need to be sitting pretty straight in front of an LCD monitor so see the full picture. Not a big issue, perhaps, but LCDs are not suited to communal viewing. Then again, does your family really sit around the PC on a regular basis?

Price Although LCD monitors are becoming more affordable, they still cost about three times more than a CRT of the same size. However, remember that a 15-inch LCD offers practically the same visible viewing area as the average 17-inch CRT when you're making comparisons. LCDs also have much lower running costs as they consume markedly less power.

There's no getting away from it: LCD monitors are infinitely sleeker and sexier than their CRT cousins.

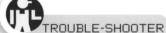
TROUBLE-SHOOTER

No picture? It sounds obvious but make sure that the monitor is plugged in *and* switched on. **Also check** that the graphics card isn't trying to produce an image at a higher resolution and/or refresh rate than the monitor can handle.
Is the brightness set to zero? It sounds unlikely but it can happen during experimentation with the monitor's own controls.
Failing that, reconnect your original monitor and see if the picture returns. If so, it's a safe bet that your new monitor is a dud – but do seek out the troubleshooting section in the manual and eliminate all possible problems before sending it back.

Installing your new monitor

On one hand, this is a simple case of switching off your PC, unplugging the old monitor, plugging in the new one, and rebooting. If you install a modern monitor, Windows will automatically detect that something has changed and launches the New Hardware Found wizard, at which point you'll be prompted to install the monitor's driver. But (you just knew there would be a but), it takes a little more effort to get a perfect picture.

Get tweaking First off, you'll want to experiment with the monitor's own controls. Modern monitors typically have a couple of buttons that control elements of the display, such as brightness, contrast and position (i.e. you can adjust the image width and depth to fill the available screen space). Most provide an onscreen display that makes it very much easier to see what you're doing.

As we've seen, the graphics card is responsible for generating the image that appears on screen, and now is the time to tweak its settings to best effect. For instance, you might want to boost the refresh rate to take advantage of your new monitor's increased capabilities. Click Start, point to Settings, click Control Panel, and then double-click Display. Under the Settings tab, you can set the resolution (screen area) and colour depth. Click the Advanced button to access further options. Be sure to check and, if necessary, adjust the refresh rate in the Adapter tab. Set it to the highest rate that your monitor can support at the resolution you've chosen (consult the manual for details). It's generally easier on the eyes to compromise with a lower resolution and a higher refresh rate than the other way around.

Play around with the display settings and any supplied utilities to make the most of your new monitor.

Dual monitor setup

Here's a smart thing. If you now have two monitors on your hands, it's possible to hook them both up to your computer and use them simultaneously. The main requirement is that you must be running Windows 98 or Millennium Edition, as Windows 95 does not support this feature. Assuming that your new monitor is powered by an AGP graphics card, you'll also need to install a PCI graphics cards to drive the second monitor. Of course, you may have just such a thing handy if you upgraded your graphics card at the same time as the monitor. Even if you don't have AGP, it's perfectly possible to run a dual monitor display on two PCI cards.

Simply install the secondary graphics card alongside the main card (follow the directions on p.78), plug in the secondary monitor, and switch on your PC. Windows will detect the new card/monitor combination and prompt for the drivers.

Now click Start, point to Settings, click Control Panel, and then double-click Display. In the Settings tab, you'll see a picture of two monitors side by side. Click on the monitor numbered 2 and click Yes when asked if you wish to enable it. Finally, position the secondary monitor to the left or right of the main monitor to match its position on your desk. Now you have a single Windows working space spread across two screens.

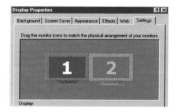

Waste not, want not. Use that old monitor to set up a dual display system.

TECHIE CORNER

Digital vs. analog
Here's a curiosity. Computers work with digital data but traditional CRT monitors require an analog input (i.e. a signal that varies continuously and smoothly over time: think of the sweeping hands of an analog clock and contrast with a digital display that jumps from second to second). Thus the graphics card must convert digital image data into an analog signal that the monitor can understand. Would it not therefore make sense to design monitors that understand digital data directly and so do away with all this translation nonsense? Yes, in a word, and the latest generation of LCD monitors do just that. However... the current crop of graphics cards are so rooted in analog technology that they can't produce a digital signal. So, in order to use a digital LCD display, you must first install either a dedicated digital graphics card or a card that supports both analog and digital output. Digital LCDs are also ferociously expensive. For more on digital displays, look here:
http://www.vesa.org
http://ddwg.org

PART **5**

Upgrading your keyboard

Have too many coffee spills made too many sticky keys? Did running your keyboard under the tap do more harm than good? Do key caps come flying off in all directions every time you type? Have you outgrown that cheap, flimsy, undersized device so clearly thrown in as an afterthought with your new computer system? Do you want some extra bells and whistles in the shape of shortcut keys and internet buttons? Or have sore wrists and the onset of RSI (Repetitive Strain Injury) driven you to consider an ergonomic approach?

What you need to know
Very little, in truth, but a few pointers won't go amiss.

Connector Keyboards generally have either a small 6-pin PS/2 connector or a larger 5-pin DIN connector at the end of their cables. Although you can buy adapters to convert one to the other, it's easier by far to source a keyboard that's immediately compatible with your PC. Alternatively, if you're running Windows 98 or ME, consider a USB keyboard. In this case, go for a model with a built-in USB hub as this allows you to connect a couple of low-powered devices (including perhaps a USB mouse) directly to the keyboard.

How do 26 letters and 10 digits add up to 100-plus keys?

If your new keyboard has the wrong connector for your case, get yourself an adapter.

Those handy Windows keys are useful shortcuts.

Key count Today's keyboards come with somewhere between 101 and 107 keys as standard. Any reference in the specifications to "Windows 95" guarantees the inclusion of three extra keys that provide quick access to the Start menu and context-sensitive menus (equivalent to a right-click with the mouse in most applications).

Ergonomics "Ergonomic" is a marketing term, not a standard and definitely not a science. That said, ergonomic keyboards are designed to maintain a more natural hand and wrist posture, thus helping to prevent symptoms of RSI such as carpal tunnel syndrome. The first time you try one, it will feel decidedly odd and distinctly *un*natural – but persevere and you'll likely be hooked. Our advice is to seek the testimony of friends and colleagues. Toying with a keyboard for thirty seconds in a shop really doesn't tell you anything.

Extras Some keyboards even have a built-in trackball which can save a lot of to-ing and fro-ing between the keyboard and the mouse. Others feature "hot keys" that provide shortcuts to programs and frequently accessed features. Look out too for clip-on wrist rests; these can help to prevent stress even on standard, flat, non-ergonomic keyboards.

Do your wrists a favour with an ergonomic design.

TECHIE CORNER

Under the (key) covers

Every modern keyboard puts a switch under each and every keycap. Keyboard makers typically use conventional metal-to-metal contacts complete with springs to push the key back once you've pressed it down or rubber domes that you squash then spring back. In either case, they can tailor the touch to be soft and gentle, springy, or snap-like. Which you prefer is a matter of taste. Try out different keyboards to find one you like.

Installing your new keyboard

It doesn't get much easier than this. Switch off your computer, unplug the old keyboard, plug in the new one, and switch the computer back on. In most circumstances, the new device will work immediately but it may take a software program to activate any special keys and functions. As always, have any disks that came with the device at hand, along with your Windows installation CD-ROM.

Color coding makes a simple job foolproof.

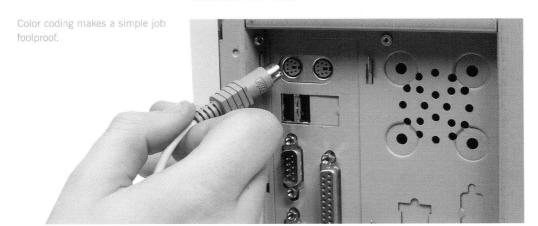

TROUBLE-SHOOTER

You're very unlikely to run into difficulties installing a keyboard. However, one possibility, albeit rare, is that you plug in a new USB keyboard, reboot, and find that you can't enter your user name or password (assuming you have password protection set up). The problem is that the USB device's driver has not yet been installed, so Windows doesn't know that the keyboard exists and thus can not recognize its commands. The workaround is to switch the PC off once more, plug in your old keyboard *while leaving the USB keyboard connected* and enter your user name and password on the old device. When Windows starts, the drivers for the USB keyboard can be installed. Next time you shut down the PC, unplug the old keyboard. You should now have no further problems. Alternatively, try clicking Cancel when the

password prompt appears. This should bypass the security feature and enable the driver to be installed.

To tweak keyboard settings, click Start, point to Settings, click Control Panel, and then double-click Keyboard. The precise options available to you depend upon the make and model of the device.

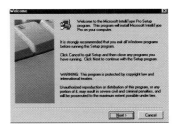

Fancier keyboards come with their own application software.

Upgrading your mouse

Cat got your mouse? Or has the poor thing just worn out? A computer mouse certainly has a finite lifespan but many people mistake a gunked-up trackball with terminal hardware failure. Have a quick glance at p.132 before consigning the poor creature to the dustbin. Otherwise, if a new mouse really is on the cards, here are the main considerations.

What you need to know

Connector Mice come with serial, PS/2 and USB connectors. In the first two cases, buy whichever is compatible with your PC – probably the same design as your current one – or be sure to get an adapter. Some of the latest, swankiest and costliest mice are USB-only.

Buttons and wheels All mice have two clickable buttons, some have three, and many now have a central wheel nestling between the left and right buttons. You may find this awkward to use at first but it's a terrific boon for scrolling swiftly through documents and web pages. Indeed, we'd unhesitatingly recommend the wheel as sufficient reason to upgrade an old mouse.

Even something as basic as a mouse comes in a wide array of fancy permutations.

Optical mice This style of modern mouse has an optical (light) sensor on its underbelly that detects its motion and relays this to the computer. No more de-fluffing but do use a mat because optical mice don't always work well on all surfaces.

Cordless mice If you keep snagging your mouse on desktop furniture, consider the wireless variety. Here, a radio sensor plugs into the mouse port and picks up signals from the roving rodent.

Trackballs Instead of sliding a mouse around a mat, a trackball stays stationary while you move the screen cursor by manipulating a big ball, just like the arcade games of yore. Some people love them; others wouldn't give them deskroom.

Extras Some mice have four, five or six buttons onboard, some of which can be individually programmed to perform common functions. These are worth considering if you tend to use the mouse more than the keyboard.

Installing your new mouse

As with a keyboard, switch off, plug it in, switch on again and away you go. Really, it's as simple as that. Well, usually…

Optical mice run fluff-free forever.

How to upgrade your mouse: plug it in!

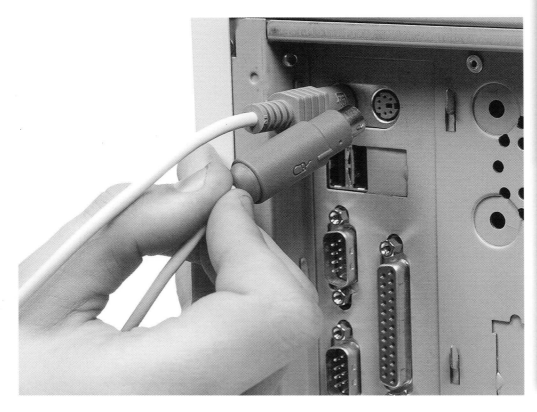

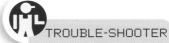
TROUBLE-SHOOTER

Windows includes a standard mouse driver that gets most devices working immediately. However, the New Hardware Found wizard might just spring into life during the first reboot, especially if you've opted for a fancy breed. If so, be ready to load the software supplied with the mouse.

Assuming that your new mouse works from the outset, install any specialist software from the supplied CD-ROM (or floppy disk) at your leisure and experiment with your new options.

To tweak mouse settings, click Start, point to Settings, click Control Panel, and then double-click Mouse. The precise options available to you depend upon the make and model of the device.

PART 5

Upgrading your speakers

Decent speakers can make even the crummiest sound card sound better than it deserves to, but a top-notch sound card is wasted on those tiny, tinny units usually bundled with a computer. So, be you music lover or musician, computer games player or DVD movie fan, invest in a decent set of speakers if you want to rock the house.

What you need to know

Hi-fi buffs will have little trouble with speaker specifications but the rest of us need a little help.

Subwoofers and satellites A subwoofer is a big-speaker-in-a-box that sits on the floor and boosts the bass signal. Satellites are smaller but still full-range speakers positioned left and right of the listener in order to produce a stereo effect. Such a setup is described as 2.1 (two satellites plus a subwoofer) or 4.1 (four satellites plus a subwoofer).

Surround sound This is the effect created when a second set of speakers is positioned behind you, one to each side, to complement a pair of stereo speakers and a subwoofer positioned in front (as in a 4.1 setup). A surround sound-capable sound card then pumps different elements of the audio signal to different speakers. The enveloping effect can be quite spooky. Look for the term 'four channel surround' or similar on your sound card spec. Game-specific standards include A3D and EAX.

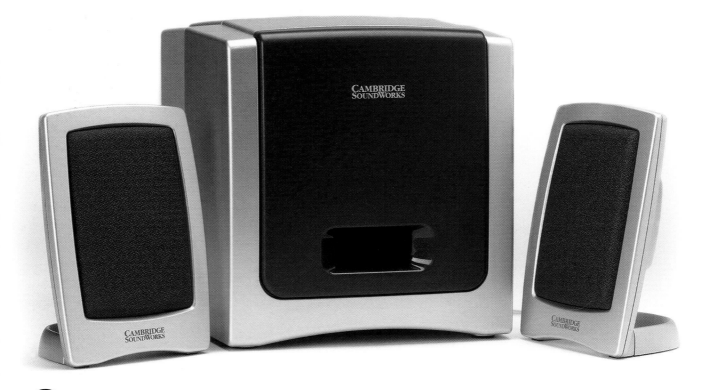

High-tech speakers need to be positioned correctly and configured with software.

Get a 4.1 speaker set up for surround sound – but only if your sound card supports it.

Home cinema Surround sound for home cinema involves yet another satellite speaker (hence 5.1) positioned directly in front of the listener. However, it needs a high-end sound card to work to full effect and this means one that supports Dolby Digital soundtracks. Stunning sound, but for DVD movie purists only.

Digital input Most sound cards and speakers work with analog signals but there is a digital breed as well. If your sound card happens to support digital output – look for the term S/PDIF, or Sony/Philips Digital InterFace – it's worthwhile getting digital speakers to complement it. Otherwise, you'll be looking at a costly sound card-plus-speakers upgrade. Is it worth it? Only your ears can answer that one.

USB Sound cards convert the digital signal from, say, an audio CD or MP3 file into an analog signal and pipe it to the speakers. However, it's now possible to buy digital speakers that connect to the PC through the USB port, bypassing the sound card completely to pick up the digital signal at source and thereby broadcast a "cleaner" signal. You have to be pretty committed to aural fidelity to spot the difference, and they're not the easiest things to configure, but we thought we ought to mention them.

Spaghetti This is what you get when you install a 4.1 or 5.1 speaker system. Be prepared to trip over more wiring than you thought possible and be sure to follow the setup directions carefully.

Installing your new speakers
Plug them in to the audio out channel(s) on your sound card, connect the power supply to a wall socket, and switch them on. Sounds too simple to be true? Well, yes and no. No, because hooking them up to your PC really is as straightforward as that. But yes, because you will certainly have to play around with both the speaker positions and the supplied software settings before you achieve Nirvana.

TECHIE CORNER

Going overboard
Computer audio technology both analog and digital continues to evolve. We haven't even touched on the scientific stuff like signal to noise ratios and frequency responses. The bottom line is this: if you really want to use your PC as a sound system, you have a wide range of choices and should research the multitude of options carefully; but if you just want a decent sound quality for playing CDs and the occasional game, a mid-range, mid-price four-channel sound card and a decent set of 4.1 surround sound speakers will blow your socks off. To find out much, much more, go here:
http://www.audioreview.com
http://www.dolby.com

PART 5

Upgrading your printer

'Free' inkjet printers are commonly included as part of the package with new computer systems. This is fine as far as it goes but it really doesn't go very far at all. Such printers tend to be bargain basement models, all but obsolete and good for only the most rudimentary, low resolution print jobs. Run off your business cards replete with jazzy logo on one of these and… well, colleagues will accept them politely but mark you down as a cheapskate amateur. And yet it's perfectly possible to buy a superb color inkjet or monochrome laser printer for not very much money at all. So, tell the salesperson to keep the giveaway and give you a discount instead and shop around for a printer that really matches your requirements.

Prints charming More on the detailed specs in a moment but do take a moment to consider why you need a printer and what you want it to do for you. The first decision is choosing between an inkjet and a laser. If crisp, clear text is paramount, then a laser printer is a must. But if you'd like some color in your life, it's got to be an inkjet.

A modern inkjet printer can produce stunning colours at a high resolution.

Some printers are geared up to print on a wide variety of media – envelopes, various paper sizes and weights, transparencies, address stickers, labels for your home-burned CDs and so forth – while others are pretty much letter and legal size or nothing. Some run on batteries for under-the-arm instant portability; others are specially designed to print photographs at near-professional quality; still others can print direct from a digital camera without a computer in sight. There really is a printer out there for every purpose and the prices just keep on falling.

What you need to know

It pays to research the market carefully and we'd read about a few comparative group tests in computer magazines to see what's currently hot and what's not. Such is the pace of evolution that last month's super-duper photo-realistic miracle of modern engineering is invariably this month's overpriced smudger. Here's a guide to the main considerations.

Interface There are two connection choices, generally speaking: the traditional parallel port or USB. Either is fine but USB might be more convenient if you already have a device wired up to the parallel port (an external Zip drive, for instance). Look for a network interface card – or at least the potential to add one – on a laser printer if you want to share it with colleagues in a workgroup.

From portable to professional, there are printers to suit every output.

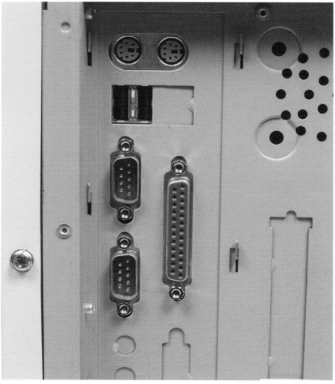

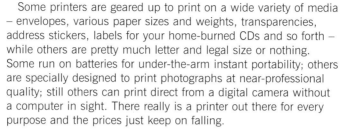

Go for a USB printer if your PC supports it.

Consumables As a rule, color inkjet printers are cheaper to buy than monochrome laser printers but more expensive to run. This is because they use one or more ink cartridges that must be replaced when they run dry. These things aren't cheap and, irritatingly, the cheapest printers often use the most expensive cartridges. Do the maths: a giveaway inkjet that costs more than its own purchase price to refill each time is not much of a bargain.

Be sure to choose a printer that uses separate black and color ink cartridges, as there's nothing more wasteful than throwing out perfectly good colors just because the black runs out (and vice versa).

Be aware that if you're tempted to *refill* old cartridges with cheap ink – and there are plenty of companies who'll happily sell you a kit to do just that – you can save a pretty penny but you'll almost certainly invalidate the printer's warranty. The print quality is also likely to be poorer.

Insist on an inkjet printer that uses separate black and colored ink cartridges.

TECHIE CORNER

Print technologies

The two grand *impact* printers of yesteryear were clattering, clumsy affairs. Dot-matrix models struck pins against an ink-impregnated ribbon – the greater the number of pins, the better the quality of the letters – while daisy-wheel machines hammered protruding characters on a rotating disk. Both are happily all but obsolete, certainly on the domestic desktop (which is not to say that you won't find them bashing out notes in warehouses around the world: if staff have to shout, there's an impact printer at work).

Laser printers use light to generate a charged image on a drum and heat-fuse powdery black toner onto paper. *Inkjet printers* squirt tiny globules of ink straight at the page. This used to mean that pages came out all sopping wet and soggy, but no longer. It's all so much more refined these days, and a good deal more flexible. Even the cheapest inkjet printer suffices for homework projects and printing out web pages, and the humblest laser can produce professional quality text. What the world is waiting for, of course, is the affordable *color* laser printer. Such things exist and are increasing in popularity but the price premium is still pretty prohibitive.

High-quality paper is a worthwhile investment for photographic reproduction.

Laser printer

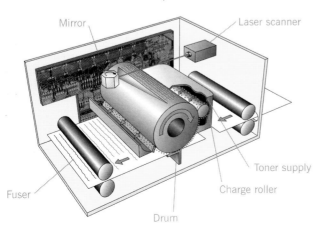

Mirror

Laser scanner

Fuser

Charge roller

Toner supply

Drum

Inkjet cartridge

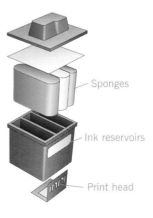

Sponges

Ink reservoirs

Print head

Resolution This is a rating of the level of detail in a printed image, measured in terms of dots per inch. Look for at least 600dpi or 1200dpi. Beware of references to 'enhanced' or 'interpolated' resolution, as this involves software sophistry and is not a true reflection of a device's ability. Also check that a quoted resolution of 600dpi means 600 x 600 (i.e. 600 dots per inch horizontally *and* vertically). Sometimes, 600 x 300 resolutions are misleadingly described as 600dpi.

Memory Laser printers have to buffer data from the PC as they work and so incorporate RAM chips. The bare minimum is 512KB but 2 or 4MB makes for faster, more reliable performance. Many models' memory can be upgraded, which could be helpful if your work rate shoots up or you print a lot of graphics.

Speed Most manufacturers claim that their printers are capable of churning out X pages of Y-sized paper with Z% ink coverage per minute. That would be just fine if they all used the same criteria, but they don't. Sadly, it's up to you to get out the calculator and do the math. However, do you really *care* how fast your printer is? Most domestic tasks are hardly 'mission critical' so we'd suggest concentrating more on quality than on speed.

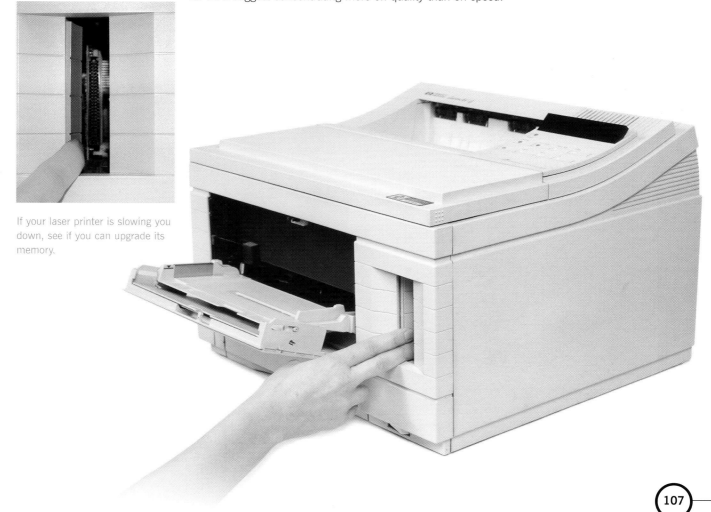

If your laser printer is slowing you down, see if you can upgrade its memory.

TECHIE CORNER

Multifunction devices

What, you may wonder, of those multifunction devices that combine a printer with a scanner with a fax machine with a copier in one neat, if rather bulky, unit? On the upside, such devices are cheaper to buy, use fewer cables and take up less space than separate components, and are thus particularly well suited to a small home office environment. However, do consider the implications if one particular element should happen to fail and the whole shebang gets sent away for repair. Will you suddenly find yourself suddenly faxless just because your printer's out of order?

MFDs (sometimes called "MFPs" for Multi-Function Printers)come in both inkjet and laser flavors, and we would strongly advise that you pay special attention to the print specifications, as this is the most central and important component. Judge an MFD primarily on the same basis that you would judge a standalone printer, and then weigh whether the additional features justify the price. Don't forget that if your PC has a modem, you can already send and receive paperless faxes.

Media Virtually all laser printers work just fine with cheap, plain paper (so-called laser paper is just a little whiter and brighter). However, it is worth investing in specialist papers to get the best results from an inkjet. Don't feel that you necessarily have to buy the printer maker's brand, though; a little experimentation with alternative papers often pays dividends.

Duty cycle This is the manufacturer's measure of a printer's maximum workload. A monthly duty cycle of, say, 12,000 pages means just that: don't print any more than 12,000 pages in any given month if you want the device to continue performing at its peak. Clearly, this has much more relevance in an office setting than at home.

Lifespan How long is a piece of string? Keep refilling an inkjet printer when it runs dry and it should last "forever" – or at least until you upgrade your operating system and discover that it no longer supports your now-obsolete device!

The photosensitive drum in a laser printer must be periodically replaced, sometimes at quite some cost. Some printer makers (such as Hewlett-Packard) make the drum and toner a single cartridge. Others make the drum a separately replaceable element. With these, look for a drum lifespan of somewhere between 15–30,000 pages, and be sure to factor this in when making price comparisons.

Printers use either the parallel or a USB port.

Software You may find a whole heap of application software in the box. Inkjets typically come with a photo editing package and something along the lines of a make-your-own-greetings-cards utility. But don't be swayed by the software alone: it's not nearly as important as the hardware specifications.

Installing a new printer

All printers have a pre-installation routine that generally involves removing strategic strips of packing tape, loading the ink cartridges or toner, bolting on a feeder and output trays, and perhaps running a self-test procedure. Follow the manual's instructions to the letter.

Thereafter, it's simply a case of connecting it to the PC's parallel or USB port. USB printers usually include the cable. You may have to buy your own parallel printer cable. Look for one marked IEEE 1284, the standard which most printers require. Windows will prompt for a USB device's driver immediately but if you're installing a parallel port device, follow these steps:

Click Start.
Click Settings.
Click Control Panel.
Double-click Printers.

Double-click Add Printer.

TROUBLE-SHOOTER

If print quality isn't up to scratch, look for and run a diagnostic program. This should be included on the installation CD-ROM. Inkjet print heads benefit from periodic cleaning but this is a process controlled by software (i.e. don't take a cotton swab to an ink cartridge).

Most printers also let you perform a rudimentary self-test just by pushing a button or two on the device itself. Consult the manual.

Does Windows know that this is the default printer i.e. the one that all applications should use without asking? Return to the Printers folder (Step 1 above) and look for a big bold check next to the appropriate icon. If it's not there, right-click the icon and select Set as Default.

Printer drivers are usually updated on a regular basis so it makes sense to visit the

manufacturer's website periodically. A new driver can often resolve bugs and glitches and may add some smart new features.

Unfortunately, printers have many moving parts and the software that turns a computer-generated digital document into a printed page is complex. In other words, lots can go wrong. The upside is that virtually all problems are easily rectified. Again, check the manual for guidance and consult the manufacturer's website.

Select your printer make and model from the list, insert the supplied CD-ROM or floppy disk in its drive, click the Have Disk button, and tell Windows which drive to look in. When the driver has been installed, you'll be instructed to reboot the PC.

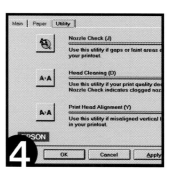

Finally, install any application programs supplied with the device. The manual may suggest that you run a print alignment utility before you start printing. Don't skip this step as it determines the accuracy of your prints.

PART  **Upgrading your scanner**

A scanner takes a picture of a piece of paper and turns it into a digital image that's viewable on your computer. There, it's as simple as that. So what might you use one for?

Well, you could scan a paper document into your PC and then fax it through the modem. Or you could print out a hard copy or two and thus emulate a photocopier. You might scan recipes, magazine articles, newspaper clippings or handwritten notes and preserve them forever on your hard disk, or perhaps email them to friends as file attachments. You could scan your snapshots, remove the red-eye and embarrassing ex-partners with an image editing program, and publish them on your website or in a newsletter. You might even scan every shred of paper in your possession and index and archive it all neatly on disk, so creating a truly paperless home/office. The uses for a scanner are indeed many and varied.

Like printers, "free" scanners are often bundled with new computers to add the illusion of value but invariably they're second-rate models. Plus any scanner more than a couple of years old is going to be vastly outclassed by today's generation.

Flatbed is the most common design for scanners. However, there are plenty of alternatives, including truly portable pen-sized models.

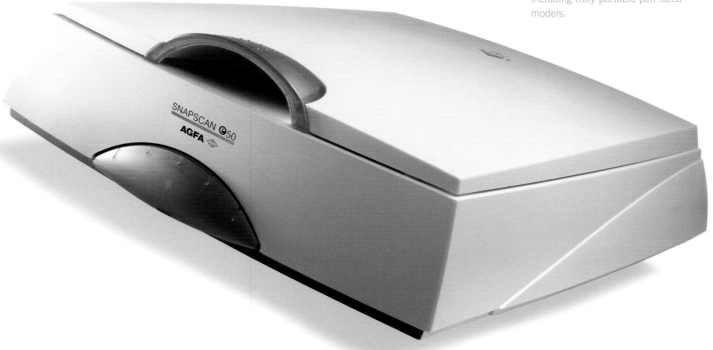

SNAPSCAN e50
AGFA

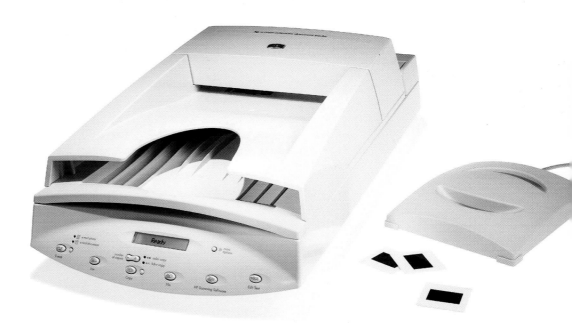

An ADF attachment saves time and effort when making multiple scans.

What you need to know

The language of scanner technology is unfamiliar to most but in fact there's nothing too complicated.

Design Scanners come in all shapes and sizes but flatbed models are by far the most popular. These look just like mini photocopiers: you lift the lid, place a document face down on the glass plate, close the lid and initiate the scan using software on your PC. Any flatbed should handle a letter size page with room to spare, and the lids are often cleverly hinged or completely removable in order that bulky objects like books can be scanned.

Alternative designs include handheld scanners that you manually sweep across the page and sheetfeed models where you feed pages through a roller mechanism one at a time.

Interface SCSI was once common but usually meant having to install an adapter on an internal expansion card, which was tricky and expensive. USB is now the interface of choice but the slower parallel port also suffices.

Resolution The detail of a scanned image is measured in terms of dots per inch. More is better. Look for at least 600 x 1200dpi true, or *optical*, resolution (as opposed to *interpolated* resolution – usually a much higher figure but not a true reflection of a scanner's capability).

Color depth This describes how many colors a scanner can distinguish. A newer term is dynamic range. Older scanners stuck at 24 bits but today the cheapest scanners boast 30 bits and good ones scan at 36 bits. New models are moving to 42 bits and even 48 bits. The greater color depths help scanners deal with bright and dark images as well as distinguish finer color variations. For scanning magazines and photos at home, a 30-bit scanner is good enough – though graphic arts workers love 42.

Twain In order for scanners to communicate with a wide range of software applications, they virtually all support a common standard called Twain (officially not an acronym but Technology Without An Interesting Name, according to urban legend). This means that even a word processor or spreadsheet program can import an image straight from a scanner.

ADF Strictly an optional extra, Automatic Document Feeders feed documents through a flatbed scanner one page at a time. Very useful for high volume work.

Transparency adapter This is a bolt-on accessory with a built-in light that enables a scanner to scan photographic transparencies.

OCR If you scanned the page that you're reading right now into your computer, you might think that you could immediately cut, copy and paste the text. But you'd be wrong. A scanned page is merely an image that makes no distinction between words and pictures. OCR, or Optical Character Recognition, is the process of turning a scanned image into editable text. Essentially, software

OCR software turns a scan into editable text.

"reads" the image and determines which bits are words (and, crucially, *which* words) and which bits are design elements and pictures. OCR is almost never 100% successful but the best programs let you proof read as you go along to correct mistakes. Most scanners come with at least a "lite" OCR package in the box.

Speed As with printers, some scanners are marginally quicker than others. The interface makes the biggest difference: SCSI scanners are quickest, parallel scanners slowest, and USB falls in the middle.

Software Look for at least a basic image manipulation program with your new toy. After all, you're going to want to tweak all those scanned images. For real ease of use, some scanners have a one-touch button that fires them into action without fussing with software. Others start working as soon as you open or close the lid. However, in most cases you'll run a Twain-compliant application on your PC and control the scanning process from there.

Installing your new scanner

You install a USB scanner in exactly the same way as any other USB peripheral: connect it to a free USB port on your PC and install the driver from the supplied CD-ROM or floppy disk when prompted. For a parallel model, close down the PC first, connect the scanner to the parallel port, switch on the scanner, reboot the computer, and follow the New Hardware Found wizard's directions.

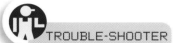

TROUBLE-SHOOTER

On the hardware front, there's nothing much to say: a scanner either works or it doesn't. Do, however, be sure to release the scan head before you make your first scan. To prevent damage in transit, it's commonplace for the scanner's moving parts (under the glass plate) to be secured with some sort of release mechanism. Check the manual for instructions.

There are usually plenty of options to play with in the application software and making a perfect scan – often a compromise between image size, resolution and colour depth – invariably takes patience and practice. Some of the best and most recent programs make scanning *almost* intuitive.

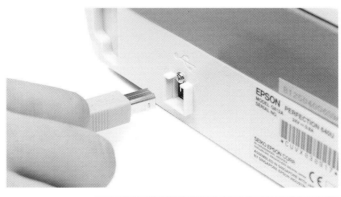

Scanners come in parallel and SCSI flavors but USB is a good compromise between speed and convenience.

6

PART **6** **PC maintenance**

Windows utilities	**116**
Third-party utilities	**122**
Viruses – a special case	**124**
Taking precautions	**126**
Cleaning your PC	**130**

Computer hardware is a curious mix of solid-state components with no moving parts to break or seize and precision-engineered, finely-tuned devices that require regular maintenance and cleaning to work at their best. Things can and do go wrong so here we consider some sensible preventative measures to stop potential problems in their tracks, some basic trouble-shooting techniques, and a maintenance regime designed to keep your PC running smoothly.

PART  Windows utilities

As you might expect, Windows (95/98/Me) comes equipped with an array of useful tools designed to optimize its own performance. While many people swear by the likes of Norton SystemWorks or McAfee Office, others never spend a penny on third-party utility software. We'll consider commercial alternatives shortly but for now let's look at what Windows itself has to offer.

Defragmenting your hard disk improves performance.

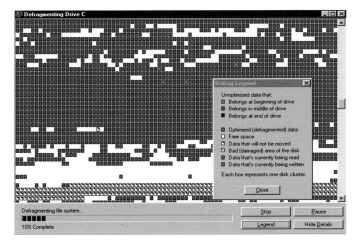

Disk Defragmenter

The data on your hard disk is stored in lots of small packets. Although this is an efficient use of space, one side effect is that individual files can get split apart and stored piecemeal all over the disk. This process is known as fragmentation and it only gets worse with time. Every time you open a fragmented file, Windows has to track down all the different bits and pieces and stick them back together again – a time-consuming and wasteful business. However, with a utility called Disk Defragmenter, you can restore all files to their former glory and speed up system performance.

Close down all programs before running Disk Defragmenter.

It's important to close down all system activity before you begin as any attempt by a program to write data to the hard disk causes Disk Defragmenter to start from scratch. Close all running programs like your word processor, browser or email program in the usual way, and disconnect from the internet. You should end up with a clear Desktop and no buttons on the Taskbar. Then look in the System Tray – the part of the Taskbar next to the clock – for icons that show which programs are running in the background. Right-click each icon in turn and select Exit or Close. You should be left with just the clock and speaker icons.

Finally, press the Ctrl, Alt and Delete keys simultaneously. This reveals any other open, but hidden, applications. Highlight each item in turn – *with the exception of Explorer and Systray* – and select Shut Down.

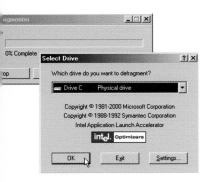

Tell the program which disk to work on.

Now click Start, Programs, Accessories and System Tools. Here you will find Disk Defragmenter. Start the program and select the drive you wish to repair (usually C: drive).

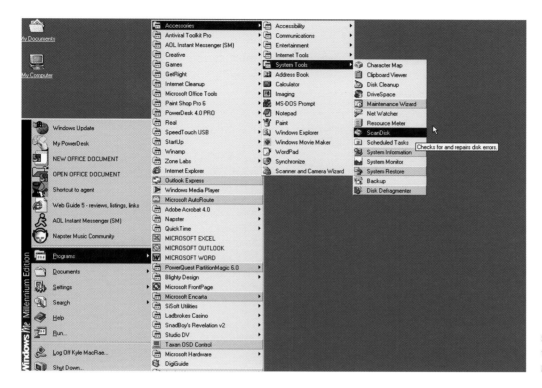

System Tools isn't the easiest
folder to find but it hosts several
good utilities.

ScanDisk

Whenever your PC crashes or closes down unexpectedly, you
may notice that it runs through an error checking process next
time you start it up. This is ScanDisk looking for, and hopefully
fixing, file problems on the hard disk. However, you can also run
ScanDisk on demand. Here's how.

Click Start, Programs, Accessories, System Tools and ScanDisk.
There are two options here: a Standard test, which is reasonably
quick and checks all your files and folders for errors; and a
Thorough test, which takes much longer but also examines the
physical integrity of your hard disk. If you're having problems
with your PC – perhaps a document won't open – the Standard
test is usually enough, but we'd recommend a Thorough scan
once in a while as part of a periodic system maintenance regime.

Check the box marked "Automatically fix errors" to speed things
up. You can set the parameters of what ScanDisk will and will not
do in the Advanced dialog box but the default options are just
fine. As with Disk Defragmenter, leave ScanDisk to work in peace.

If it finds any lost clusters (parts of files), it saves them with the
extension .CHK in the root directory (the topmost folder in
Windows). These may safely be deleted. If, however, ScanDisk
reports any "bad sectors," back-up your files immediately.
Although Windows will not now write any new data to these
unusable areas of the hard disk, it may be a sign of impending
disk failure.

Let ScanDisk automatically fix any
problems it finds.

Disk Cleanup

Programs take up a lot of space but so can individual files, particularly web pages saved to the hard disk by your web browser. Disk Cleanup can automatically remove a good deal of this debris.

As with Disk Defragmenter and ScanDisk, Disk Cleanup is found in the System Tools menu. The program offers several options: simply check each box in turn for an explanation of what it does. Do be cautious about emptying the Recycle Bin, especially if you've just deleted a bunch of files. Murphy's Law assures you'll wish you hadn't permanently consigned that complete record of your household finances to oblivion three seconds after you push the button.

The Temporary Internet Files section may be quite large. This is your browser's cache – an area of your hard disk set aside for keeping copies of the web pages you visit. If you delete its contents, your browser will have to reload each page from scratch next time you revisit a favorite site instead of plucking some or all of its elements from the cache. This may slow down your surfing a little but the cache soon fills up again and the effects are short-lived. Besides, many web pages are updated frequently so having an old copy on your computer isn't really much of an advantage.

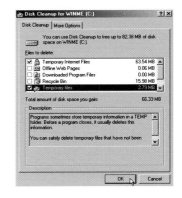

Disk Cleanup explains what it's going to do before it starts.

Don't let rubbish clog up your hard disk.

Maintenance Wizard

The problem with ScanDisk, Disk Defragmenter and Disk Cleanup is, of course, that you'll never remember to use them. That's why Windows includes Maintenance Wizard, a utility that lets you set up an automatic schedule for running one, two or all three programs at regular intervals. Once again, find it by clicking Start, Programs, Accessories and System Tools, and then run Maintenance Wizard in custom mode. Note that it's best to schedule these tasks to run at a time when you're not using your computer, like the middle of the night. You also have to ensure that no running programs will interfere with Disk Defragmenter (see above), so close down anything that's not absolutely essential and deactivate any screensaver before you bed down. Oh, and don't forget to leave your computer switched on and running.

If you're prone to forgetfulness, what you want is a Wizard.

Drive Converter

If you're still obstinately running Windows 95 and refuse to upgrade, far be it for us to question your choice. However, you might at least care to consider a simple way of improving the way in which Windows manages your disk space.

In Windows 95, the minimum unit of file storage (called a cluster) is 32 kilobytes. This means that a saved 10K file, for example, effectively wastes 22K of disk space. However, there are two options to improve this state of affairs. First, if your hard disk is smaller than 500MB, Windows automatically switches to a more efficient 4K cluster size. (Even if your disk is bigger than 500Mb, you could partition it into smaller segments and thus fool Windows into treating each partition as a separate disk.)

Alternatively, convert your filing system to the vastly more efficient FAT32 system with Drive Converter, a Windows 95b and 98 utility located in the System Tools menu. This utility is not available in Window Me, XP, or the NT family (including Windows 2000). To check if you have Window 95a or 95b, click Start, Settings, Control Panel, System and look in the General tab of System Properties. If your version of Windows 95 ends with the letter *a*, you're out of luck.

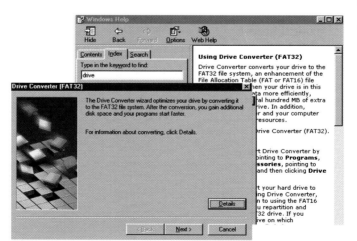

Changing to the FAT32 file system improves disk management in Windows 95.

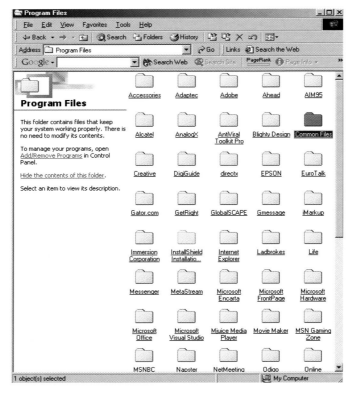

How many of your programs do you actually use?

Add/Remove Programs

Ah, if only life was simple and you could install and delete software at will and with ease. Well, sometimes you can, but only sometimes. The trouble is that there's no single, catch-all, foolproof method for ridding a system of unwanted applications. Some come with their own uninstall utilities while others rely on Windows to do the work. Still others display a thoroughly leech-like determination to never be deleted.

One of the requirements for a product to carry the "Designed for Windows 95" logo on the box is compliance with Microsoft's InstallShield standard. A "true" Windows program should install smoothly and do away with itself just as easily. However, in practice, bits and pieces of programs are often left behind, notably empty folders and scattered cryptic files. Most worrying are orphaned entries in the Windows Registry, a record of all that makes your system tick. Conflicts and confusion in here can be serious.

But why bother getting rid of old software? Why not just let it be? Three reasons:

1 Old programs take up disk space. Sooner or later, you're liable to need it, so it's better to manage this as you go along

2 You might not realize it but many programs run continuously in the background even if you never actually use them to do anything useful. This eats into available RAM and has a detrimental effect on performance

3 Every additional program on your system increases the risk of a conflict with another, more useful program. As a rule, tidy systems run more smoothly, and you may find that simply uninstalling some half-forgotten software miraculously cures no end of unexplained ills

Deletion Completion

So, click Start and Programs and see just what you've got onboard. Point at any superfluous programs and see if an Uninstall option appears. If so, select it and follow the step-by-step instructions. At the end of the process, you may be warned that some elements of the program must be manually removed. Make a note of any details supplied. The leftovers are usually a top-level folder in the Program Files menu and perhaps one or two sub-folders within. Now click My Computer, select your hard disk, click Program Files and find the folder(s) that you jotted down. These may now be dragged straight to the Recycle Bin. Incidentally, Windows Millennium Edition has the less-than-endearing habit of refusing you access to Program Files on pain of the sky falling in. Just override it.

Where a program doesn't come with its own uninstaller, click Start, Settings, Control Panel and Add/Remove programs. This brings up a list of programs that Windows can automatically delete. Just highlight the program and click Add/Remove.

Some programs thoughtfully have their own uninstall option.

Add/Remove Programs clears out the clutter. Unfortunately, it doesn't always work perfectly.

PART 6 Third-party utilities

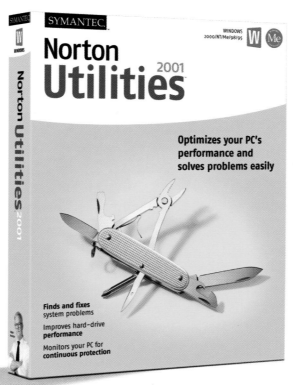

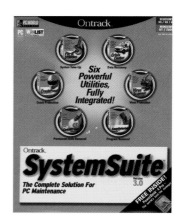

The shelves of your local computer superstore are stacked with commercial utility software that promises to make amends for the failings of Windows and keep your PC running in tip-top condition for ever and a day. Bold claims indeed, and not wholly without merit. With all such packages, there is a significant overlap with Windows' own utilities and, in the case of the major suites, often some internal features overlap as well. But the real point of these programs is threefold:

1 Routine maintenance tasks like defragmenting a hard disk and trouble-shooting hardware conflicts are faster, more efficient and above all easier to manage than with Windows alone.

2 You get value-added extra features in the bargain (see below).

3 Peace of mind. You don't have to be paranoid to believe that sooner or later your computer will self-destruct and take with it all your precious data, or that hackers will break into your system, steal your credit card number and make merry with your money. There's a good deal more hype than substance in these scare stories but the bottom line is that people feel safer with added security measures in place.

The kitchen sink approach The big players in the utility software stakes are Norton (a division of Symantec), McAfee (a division of Network Associates) and Ontrack. All three produce fully-fledged utility suites that bundle all their many programs together and offer the best overall value for money. All three also offer a range of standalone products that specialize in particular areas and offer enhanced tools. We are not inclined to recommend any one product over any other, or indeed to say that you absolutely *need* any utility software at all. But here's a quick rundown on the central features to look out for when shopping around. Note that all utilities slow your system down to some extent but that's your trade-off for added stability.

Trouble-shooting It's usual to find a "one-click-solves-all-problems" button in utility suites these days, and certainly you can save a great deal of time and effort by letting smart software seek out and resolve your system conflicts. Hardware and software issues alike can be treated, including deep-rooted Windows problems.

Crash protection A utility that stops an impending crash in its tracks and gives you the chance to save your work is worth its weight in gold. Unfortunately, results tend to be variable.

Program uninstaller Dedicated program uninstallers that do a thorough job of deleting old software.

Zip utility What better way to save disk space and tidy up than by compressing multiple files into one much smaller file, called an "archive"? Zips are commonly used on the internet to reduce the duration of file transfers. Download the evaluation version of WinZip before splashing out elsewhere: **www.winzip.com**.

Disk imaging This is the process of copying an entire hard disk in one move, up to and including the operating system, in order to load it on another computer or to recover the current system in the event of a disaster.

Firewall A program that stops hackers from gaining access to your computer.

Web services Look for a feature that scans your system to see what software you have installed and automatically finds any available upgrades, patches and bug fixes.

Encryption Want to keep your email or documents on your hard disk files secret? Then you'll be wanting a file encryption tool.

File recovery Deleted an important document by mistake? File recovery utilities can (sometimes) help.

And then, of course, there's anti-virus software. But that, we strongly suggest, is not an optional extra. Read on...

See what's going on under the hood.

Programs keep crashing? Utility software can help save your work.

Many utilities do much the same as Windows, but usually rather better.

A full utility suite may have 20 or 30 separate programs.

Viruses – a special case

Update your anti-virus software frequently.

However you cut it, computer viruses are a fact of life. At best, they're a hassle; at worst, downright destructive. You have to be something of a moron to release one "in the wild," so to speak, but there's no shortage of them in the world. And so all we can do is accept that viruses are with us in abundance and take adequate precautions.

Protect and survive

Viruses are basically programs like any other. They typically have two parts: a means of getting into your system, and a reason for doing so. Once inside, a successful virus might scramble your data, sit quietly in the background doing nothing at all until triggered by a key date, or instantly email copies of itself to everyone in your address book. Some viruses are created by geeks for the supposed kudos of being clever with code; others are written by malicious saboteurs bent on wreaking havoc across company networks or the internet itself. In all cases, your first and necessary line of defense is to install an anti-virus program. This attempts to identify inbound nasties in one or both of two ways: by spotting and isolating known viruses (highly effective but not much use against brand new bugs that aren't yet in its database); and by looking for suspiciously virus-like behavior (a good safety net, although far from foolproof).

If you suspect you've been infected, scan your system without delay.

Moreover, because new viruses appear all the time, you must update your anti-virus program regularly. If it has an auto-update feature, all to the good: allow it to call home for updates whenever you're online. Otherwise, make an appointment with yourself to manually update it *at least* once a month, and preferably once a week. Some developers now release daily updates. Remember – an out of date anti-virus program is next to worthless, so don't assume that you're safe just because your new computer came with an anti-virus program pre-installed.

Don't be fooled by silly hoaxes – check them out on the web.

Get wise to hoaxes

Equally important is making sure that you don't contribute to the spread of these pests yourself. Never pass on a virus warning without first checking whether or not it's a hoax. If a rampant email virus can bring a network to a standstill, a flurry of hoax warnings is almost as damaging. So, if you get a virus warning in your email inbox, pause and consider before forwarding it to anybody else. Does it exhort you in the strongest possible terms to tell everybody you know "WITHOUT DELAY!!!!"? Does it proclaim that unspeakable things will happen to your hard disk if you get infected? Does it read like the work of an idiot trying to get a rise out of the world? Then it's almost certainly a hoax. Check it out at Vmyths.com (**http://vmyths.com**) before you pass it on.

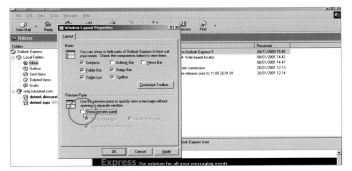

Switch off the Preview Pane option in your email program for better security.

Scan your computer for viruses on the web with McAfee.

Periodically check for Windows updates and install any security patches.

Sensible steps

Aside from installing and updating anti-virus software, there are various things you can do to minimize the risk of infection.

Switch on your anti-virus program's background scanning features to ensure that all files are checked when they are opened.

Check for security updates and patches for your email program. If you use Microsoft's Outlook or Outlook Express, go here: **http://windowsupdate.microsoft.com**

Don't download files from strangers on the internet, and delete, without opening, any unasked for email attachments. Don't even sneak a peek at mystery messages in your email program's Preview Pane, as this alone can be enough to do the damage. For maximum security, switch off the Preview Pane option altogether. In Outlook Express, click Layout in the View menu and uncheck the Preview Pane option.

Be wary of Word documents (files with the extension .DOC) and Excel spreadsheets (extension .XLS), as these could harbour macro viruses.

Never open an executable file type unless and until you've scanned it for viruses *and* been personally assured by the sender that it's safe. Extensions to look out for include: .EXE, .VBS and .JS.

Don't beg, steal or borrow software of unknown origin.

Beware of files that try to hide their true extension e.g. BritneySpearsNaked.jpg.vbs. Many a mug would assume that this is a harmless image file but the .VBS extension gives the game away: it's a script virus.

If you don't already have an anti-virus program up and running, give your system a quick health check online with McAfee Clinic: **http://www.mcafee.com**

PART  **Taking precautions**

A lightning strike could fry your computer – so better get protected!

A little foresight and rudimentary background knowledge about the various things that can do a computer system harm goes a long way towards averting serious problems. We covered static electricity at the very outset and we'll take the liberty of assuming that you already know that water and electricity don't mix (i.e. don't play with your PC in the bath). Here are some other essentials.

Magnetism

If it wasn't for the magic of magnetism, your PC's hard disk couldn't permanently store data. Nor could floppy or Zip disks transfer files from here to there and back again. But while magnetism is undoubtedly a force for good, it can also do inordinate damage to your data when allowed to interfere with the strictly controlled conditions present in your computer system. It pays, therefore, to be aware that magnets *in any form* and data stored on magnetic media (as opposed to optical media like CD-ROMs and DVD discs) do not come into contact with one another.

For instance, never stick a magnetic paper clip holder on your PC case lest it interfere with the workings of the hard disk. Keep floppies well away from magnetic sources like printers, fridges, cars, mobile phones, hi-fi speakers – and, of course, plain

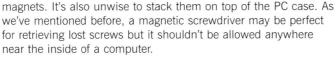

Degaussing your monitor clears up odd screen effects caused by stray magnetism.

Surge protectors are often built into power strips but be sure to get one with a warning light.

magnets. It's also unwise to stack them on top of the PC case. As we've mentioned before, a magnetic screwdriver may be perfect for retrieving lost screws but it shouldn't be allowed anywhere near the inside of a computer.

Speakers designed for use with a computer are usually shielded in order to prevent (most of) the magnetic field from interfering with the system. But if you sit them too close to a CRT monitor, they can affect the flow of electrons that makes up the display image. The result is often patches of light, dark or odd colors on the screen, and this can cause permanent damage if left unchecked. It's also prudent to keep your monitor some distance away from the main PC case to prevent any possible interference between its own magnets and the hard disk.

However, a short-term problem is easily resolved by "degaussing" the monitor to realign the magnetic fields. There may be a degauss button on the monitor itself or you may find an option in any utility software that came with the monitor. Check the manual for details.

Power surges

You may well have a good idea of just how regular, or smooth, your electricity supply is. Then again, you may have no idea. Peaks and dips are sometimes made evident by an unexpected brightening or dimming of the lights, but a *serious* peak, or spike, can do a computer serious damage.

Now, all reputable PC manufacturers build some form of surge protection into the power supply controlling the current that flows into the system but it's unwise to rely on this alone. If you consider that you're at risk from sudden voltage spikes, or if you simply want an added layer of protection, consider a heavy-duty surge protector. This is a box filled with special electrical components you plug in between your computer and the electricity supply that stops any spike in its tracks.

There are several different designs but the most effective deploy several metal-oxide varistors (MOVs) that short-out surges and thus keep your PC out of harm's way. Unfortunately, MOVs wear out over time and a single large surge may kill an MOV outright. This is fine – after all, it's the job of a surge protector to take the bullet for your computer – but, rather bizarrely, some units don't actually tell you when the MOV is dead. To avoid an unwarranted sense of security, be certain to buy a surge protector with a warning light that clearly displays whether or not it's working!

The most dramatic power surge of all is, of course, a lightning strike, and here again it pays to be protected. The first thing to do at the first sign of a storm is to switch off and unplug the computer from the wall. Don't forget the cable linking the modem to the telephone socket, as lightning will be only too happy to follow a path through the telephone wiring to your PC's motherboard, leaving you with a fried system, a daunting repair bill, and quite possibly a small electrical fire. Please don't follow the example of one hapless consumer who waited patiently for Windows to shut down correctly while the wrath of the gods unfurled in the skies above.

A UPS unit keeps you going – for a while – when the power fails.

Power outages

Spikes aren't the only power problem to afflict the computer user. Who hasn't experienced a sudden power cut and lost a minute, an hour or a day's work in a flash? Such incidents generally prove a great crash course in the importance of saving your work regularly as you go along but it's a lesson we could all do without. The answer is to invest in an uninterruptible power supply (UPS) of some sort. A UPS is essentially a battery that your utility power keeps charged so that it can take over power supply duties the instant a power outage occurs. Different models offer different levels of protection – some may provide only a few minutes power while others can keep a PC running for an hour or two (plenty of time to leap out of bed in the middle of the night, drive to the office and salvage that vital company backup job) – but the principle is simply to give you sufficient time to save your work and close down the computer in an orderly manner.

So, next time you're doing something *really* important with your PC, consider the implications if the power was suddenly to fail and use that as the basis on which to decide whether or not a UPS is warranted. Then again, if you never do anything that could be remotely construed as important or mission-critical with your computer, save your money. Incidentally, the better UPS units have surge protection features too, so what better way to kill – or rather save – two birds with one stone?

On or off?

Most of us probably switch off our PC when we're finished with it and fire it up afresh the next time we need it. But have you considered that all this off- and on-ing might actually stress its components? Opinion is sharply divided on this matter. Some people swear by leaving a computer on around the clock, day after day, month after month, and it's true that modern hardware is built to run continuously at a carefully regulated temperature. Certainly, the chances of a drive failing are much higher when spinning up or down, and how would you like being brought up to operating temperature in just a few seconds if you'd been left in a bitterly cold room all weekend? But to many it just seems counter-intuitive and wasteful to leave a machine running when it's not in use. It's really a personal judgment call more than a case of right or wrong, but do bear the following points in mind:

Don't switch your computer off and on more than absolutely necessary. Note that *warm* booting your PC (hitting the reset switch or using the Ctrl-Alt-Delete keyboard combination to restart the system) doesn't count: it's cold booting (using the main power switch) that allegedly does the damage

Don't leave your PC running unless you have a good surge protection system in place

Do use your PC's power saving features to reduce energy drain. In particular, set the monitor to switch off after a few minutes inactivity and the hard disk to go into 'sleep' mode after perhaps an hour's idleness

Do ensure that any computer connected to a network has adequate protection against hackers. You don't want your documents to disappear while you doze.

If your PC has power-saving features, it makes sense to use them.

Switching off your PC feels like the right thing to do but it's not strictly necessary.

TECHIE CORNER

Don't let the techies get you down
We're the first to say that calling a technical support telephone service should be a last resort, not your first port of call (not least because you typically pay through the nose and by the minute for such services). But if you have to seek professional help, be prepared to give a full and clear description of the apparent problem and make sure that you're by your PC. Technical support lines are (on the whole) manned by sympathetic and helpful professionals, but they are not (on the whole) mind-readers: help them to understand what's gone wrong and they'll be better placed to help you.

And before you call, remember this (probably apocryphal) story. One hapless individual phoned technical support to complain that the document she had been working on had just disappeared on her screen. The engineer ran through the usual gamut of possible problems and, baffled, finally asked her to check the cables around the back of her computer – just in case. She retorted that it was too dark to see and, no, she couldn't switch on the light because of the power failure. The techie's sage advice? Return the system to the shop and ask for a full refund on account of being far too stupid to own a computer.

Cleaning your PC

Keeping your computer clean won't make it run faster or crash less frequently, but it will:

Minimize the risk of passing germs and bugs from one user to another

Reduce the chance of over-heating and short-circuits

Make it look better

Just two words of warning. Don't go slopping around with a big wet sponge: your computer may come up smelling of roses but it most definitely won't work. And, of course, if you leave it plugged in while you clean, you may not live long enough to see the results. So unplug everything now, give yourself space and time enough to work in comfort, roll up your sleeves – and let's begin.

Surface cleaning

It's safe to clean pretty much every surface area with a dilute mixture of water and detergent, including the PC case, the monitor housing and all your peripherals. However, use only a *barely damp* cloth, avoid any exposed areas like printer parts and drive bays, and don't touch glass areas like the monitor screen or

A specialist cleaning fluid makes light work of spring cleaning.

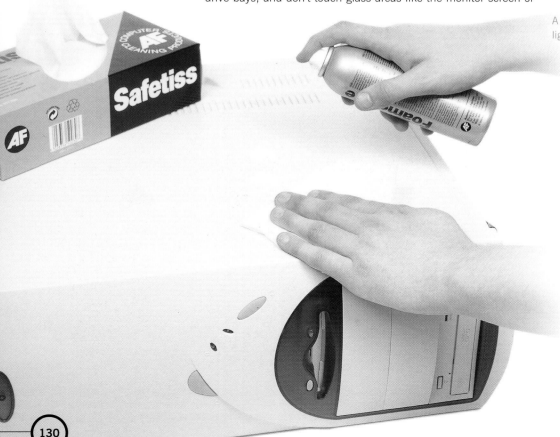

A fluffy fan can lead to overheating so always make sure that it's clean.

scanner plate. If you come across a circuit board, steer *well* clear. For better results, at a price, invest in a can of computer cleansing fluid, foam or mousse. This can cut through the grease and grime in a flash.

Pay particular attention to the protective grill that protects the main ventilation fan (around the back of the PC case), as a clogged grill reduces the flow of air to the fan and increases the risk of over-heating. Carefully but thoroughly tease out the fluff. Tweezers or a toothbrush (preferably an old one, or at least not your own) can help here.

Monitor

Some people are drawn like moths to candles to touch monitor screens with sticky fingers – we don't know why – but, they invariably leave greasy fingerprint trails behind as evidence. Why others contrive to sneeze all over their screens is another mystery, but we won't dwell on what *they* leave behind. Smoke, too, is drawn to monitors through static electricity and can soon come to coat the screen with a fine, filthy film.

To rid yourself of such stuff, the light dusting with a dry cloth recommended in the monitor's manual is unlikely to suffice. However, the screen is delicate indeed and any ammonia-based cleanser will completely destroy its protective coating. So, we strongly suggest that you purchase a specialist screen cleaner, preferably one with anti-static properties that helps reduce the further build up of muck. Be sure to use a lint-free cloth.

Be very, very careful when cleaning your screen! Only use a dry cloth or materials designed specifically for the job.

Clean out the innards of your mouse for jitter-free operation.

Keyboard and mouse

Keyboards are great collectors of crumbs, hair, dust, flaky skin, dandruff and spillages of all descriptions. You can usually shake some of this detritus clear by simply turning it upside down but there's a risk that bits will accumulate under the key caps. In time, this can affect the smooth operation of the keyboard. A better bet is to vacuum the dirt away with a small vacuum cleaner such as a Dust Buster. Some models come with nozzle attachments that let you get right between the keys and tug at the heart of the trouble. (See Under the Cover, opposite, for vacuuming hints.)

One remarkably common computer complaint is that the onscreen cursor starts jerking around when once it ran smoothly. This is a sure sign of a gummed-up mouse. Look on its underside for a retaining ring. Unscrew this and remove the ball. Now you should see three little rollers, probably entwined with fibres and fluff. Clean these carefully with a toothbrush and blow away any loose particles. Now give the ball a quick wipe and reassemble the rodent. Hey presto – one good-as-new mouse and no sticking cursor.

You may also care to spray or wipe the keyboard and mouse with an anti-bacterial solution to prevent any risk of cross-infection. Some microbacteria survive longer than others away from the human body but there is a risk (largely theoretical, it should be said) that hardware could harbor a bug long enough to pass from one hand to another and, potentially, into the bloodstream through an open cut.

A blast of compressed air is better than a shake.

Peripherals

Peripheral devices come in so many shapes and sizes that it's impossible to generalize. However, it's safe to clean a scanner's glass plate in the same way as a monitor screen (although, being under cover for most of its life, it's likely to need little more than a dusting). Your vacuum or compressed air can also clear out gunk from a printer's recesses. Most open up in one way or another, at least to provide access to the ink cartridge or toner areas, so do clean where you can. As always, read the manual for specific guidance.

Under the covers

Your computer's ventilation fan sucks air into the case but also, unfortunately, anything that happens to be floating around at the time. Most systems benefit from an internal spring cleaning once or twice a year, but – and it's a big but – you have to be careful. A domestic vacuum cleaner is expressly *not* suited to the job, and even a hand-held battery-powered version must be handled with care. One stray bump could mean a hefty repair bill.

As always, take safety precautions (see p.33) before lifting the lid and don't fry anything with static electricity. Now survey the scene. Are your expansion cards thick with dust? If so, there's an increased risk of short-circuits. Blast away the dust with a can of compressed air or *very* gently suck it up with a vacuum. *Don't* blow, as even the tiniest drop of saliva on your breath could cause a short-circuit. And don't follow the example of the well-meaning but dim owner who cleaned her computer's innards with a lather of hot, soapy water.

Check the cooling fan or heatsink unit protecting the processor and carefully free it of any obstructions. Also check and clean the main ventilation fan and any secondary fans elsewhere in the case. If you're feeling bold, you might even remove the expansion cards one by one, gently wipe their connecting surfaces and blow or suck away any accumulated dust from the slots.

Don't try this at home

Never attempt to dismantle your monitor! You'll merely invalidate the warranty and it will never work again. Oh, yes. The high voltages inside could also kill you.

Don't eat, drink or smoke near your PC unless you're prepared to wipe up the inevitable spillages, de-crumb the keyboard and otherwise clean up after yourself on a regular basis.

Always remember that water and electricity don't mix. Allow hardware to dry completely after even the quickest wipe from a damp cloth before switching it back on.

And if you really can't be bothered with any of this palaver right now, don't worry. When your once-beige PC turns grey, your monitor display is impenetrable to the naked eye, and your printer's pictures take on a sandy quality from all the accumulated dust within the device, we'll see you sporting those rubber gloves yet.

Treat all glass in the same way – with great care!

Expansion cards will thank you for a puff of compressed air.

PART 7

Trouble-shooting

Trouble-shooting in general 136
Trouble-shooting specific problems 138

Although it's certainly true that your computer system is on a fast-track to obsolescence almost as soon as you get it home from the store, the good news is that hardware reliability these days is generally very high. Today's inkjet printer should still be technically capable of churning out full color pages long after the manufacturer stops making the ink cartridges it requires. Also, most problems are evident immediately rather than, say, six months down the line. A new processor either works or it doesn't work: it doesn't *sort of* work. (For just this reason, incidentally, an expensive extended warranty is usually a waste of money.) You may be lucky and never experience a hardware problem; then again, your shiny new PC may be dead on arrival. Here we look at how to begin the trouble-shooting process.

PART

Trouble-shooting in general

The first and entirely natural reaction to a computer problem is often one of panic, compounded by the realization that we haven't been quite as rigorous with our backing up regime as we might have been. What happens if it never works again? Have all our files and documents disappeared forever? It's at such moments that we wish we had a) taken a college course in advanced computing; and b) never become so reliant upon the infernal contraption in the first place.

Checklist

But just relax. Have a cup of coffee. Go for a walk or sleep on it. Then calmly, rationally and logically think through the problem. Here are six simple steps that just might resolve your woes:

1 Are your PC and all its peripherals plugged in and switched on? How about any switches on the cases – could these have been inadvertently knocked to the off position? Be sure to check the power supply too – could a fuse have blown somewhere, either in the main fuse box or in the device's own plug? Perhaps your surge protector has given up the ghost and cut the power as a safety precaution? Many a call to technical support – and a resulting red face – could have been spared by these simplest of all checks.

Updated drivers can cure many known problems so check the manufacturer's website.

Download **Library**

Scanners

Search for a specific Scanner:

1. Select Scanner:	2. Choose Operating system:	3. Find drivers
EPSON Expression 1640XL ▾	All ▾	Search

(i) Click here for help with downloading.

Miscellaneous scanner drivers & utilities:

PC | **Parallel port test utility (60 KB)**
This ZIP file contains a utility program designed to test a PC parallel port for use with EPSON scanners. Use this program to determine if your parallel port supports true 8 bit bi-directional access. For details on usage consult the readme file supplied with the program. File name Partest.zip (updated 17/01/96) | Download

PC | **Scan Server Software for GT-9600/10000/10000+/12000, Expression 1600/1640XL (699 KB)**
This file contains the Network Scanner application Scan Server. Suitable for Windows 95, 98, Me, NT4 and 2000. File Name: scansrv.exe, Version: 1.2a (updated 19/04/01) | Download

PC | **Smart Panel Update for Perfection 1240/1640SU (2.5MB)**
This patch will allow scanned images to printed via any printer. Suitable for Windows 95, 98, 2000. File Name: copier1016-E.exe, Version: 1.1 (updated 14/11/2000) | Download

2 Check that all cables are in place. It may mean crawling around behind your system but it's not uncommon for a USB cable to fall out of its socket and render a device inoperative.

3 When did your PC or the suspect peripheral last work without trouble? Can you undo any changes that you've made in the meantime? Hardware conflicts (see Techie Corner on p.141) are common and temporarily uninstalling a newly connected component can often fix a problem or at least pinpoint its probable cause. Poorly written software applications are also notorious for thoroughly confounding the most carefully arranged system settings.

4 If you're running Windows Millennium Edition, try the System Restore utility. This is a way of reverting the computer's configuration settings to an earlier, less problematic time.
Click Start
Click Programs
Click Accessories
Click System Tools
Click System Restore.
　Now check to see when Windows made its last 'checkpoint' and let it undo any system changes between then and now. Don't worry about your files and documents: these are unaffected by System Restore. If you're lucky, problem solved: all you have to do is work out what you did in the interim to cause all the bother. If not, try an earlier checkpoint.
　Incidentally, it's well worth making your own checkpoints using System Restore before installing new software or adding hardware, just in case you want to reverse the changes in a hurry.

System Restore can take you back in time to a point before your troubles began.

5 Don't forget to read the manual! There's no better place to find device-specific help, and you'd be surprised at just how many potential problems are unique to one particular peripheral. In these cost-conscious days, chances are that the full manual (as opposed to that wafer thin "quick installation guide" that fell out of the box) is an electronic file rather than a proper printed affair. It may have been installed on your PC when you first loaded the software or you may have to find it on the installation CD-ROM.

6 Finally, if your PC is working and you have an internet connection, pay a visit to the manufacturer's website. Quite possibly, the fault that you're currently experiencing is well known and a cure is already on-hand in the form of a downloadable software "patch" or bug-fixer. You'd think they'd tell you about this, especially if you registered your product when you first acquired it, but we've lost track and count of important – even essential – bug fixes slipped quietly onto support websites without any fanfare whatsoever.

PART 7

Trouble-shooting specific problems

It's obviously beyond this manual's scope to cover every hardware eventuality. Indeed, it's beyond the scope of *any* manual, even those daunting 1,000+ page tomes that claim to teach you how to build a PC from scratch (but not necessarily how to switch it on). However, here are a handful of the more common problems to afflict the average computer system.

Hard disk

Insufficient disk space If Windows tells you that there's insufficient disk space to complete an operation or to save a file, you need to clear out some clutter. See p.121 for tips on uninstalling old software and making more space. Better still, pre-empt the problem now. Click My Computer, right-click on C: drive, and select Properties. If the disk is more than 75% full, it's time to start making economies.

Permanently busy If your hard disk appears to be permanently busy (lots of whirring noise and a constantly blinking light on the PC's case), chances are you don't have enough system memory and Windows is using the disk as a RAM substitute. Add more memory (see p.44).

Unexpected disk noises – buzzes, squeals or clicks – may be a sign of impending failure. Backup your work onto removable media (recordable CDs, Zip disks, a tape drive or similar) immediately *before* switching off your PC, and seek professional advice.

Optical drives

CD won't eject? Restart the PC and try again. If the tray still won't open, *switch off the powe*r, flatten out a paperclip and poke it into the small hole on the drive's case to release the mechanism.

Problem CDs If one particular CD won't work properly, perhaps sticking during playback or freezing the system, try cleaning it with a soft cloth. If it's scratched, it's probably irreparable, although it's certainly worth trying to run it in somebody else's computer before giving up hope. If, however, you start experiencing problems with many or all your CDs, the drive itself has a problem. Buy a lens cleaning disc to clear internal dust.

Suddenly no sound from your audio or multimedia CDs? Check the PC's volume settings are not muted (double-click the loudspeaker icon near the clock in the Windows System Tray and/or run any sound card diagnostic software). If this doesn't work, the audio cable connecting the drive to the sound card has probably become detached. Open up the case (after taking all the usual precautions – see p.33) and reattach it.

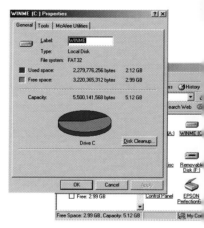

If your disk is getting full, now is the time to start making economies.

Turn to your sound card's diagnostic utilities to trouble-shoot audio problems.

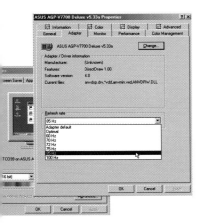

Set the refresh rate as high as your graphics card and monitor will allow.

DVD disc won't play? Check that it has the same regional code as your DVD drive (see p.66). Windows itself – except for Windows XP – can't play DVD movies so you need a DVD player program. Do you have one installed?

Monitors

Unusual patches of color on the screen, especially near the edges, are probably due to some magnetic influence or a heavy piece of iron or steel near the screen. Use the degauss button or software utility to remove excess magnetism and move any magnetic sources – including speakers and the PC case itself – further from the monitor.

Flickering If you can see any flickering in the screen image, the refresh rate is too low. This is a certain way to develop a headache while using your computer. See p.92 and make sure that the refresh rate is set to at least 72Hz (or higher if your monitor supports it).

TECHIE CORNER

Disk disaster

Hard disks don't last for ever (although most are still spinning quite happily come the time for an upgrade) but, short of a catastrophe such as complete destruction or theft, it's almost always possible to recover data from a badly damaged disk. Many companies worldwide specialize in data recovery, and some will even attempt a diagnosis through a modem link. The problem is that professional data recovery is always an expensive option. That's why it pays to archive your old data on Zip disks, recordable CDs, tape or even floppy disks.

However, if you simply must recover current data, the procedure depends upon the severity of the problem. If you've accidentally deleted the odd file or reformatted an entire disk and now wish you hadn't, or if a virus wreaked havoc, specialist software alone can sometimes recover your data. In the case of physical damage, a disk that's still working from an electro-mechanical point of view – i.e. still spinning – is relatively easy to work with, but even a device badly damaged by a power surge or fire can sometimes be persuaded to yield usable data. Not one to try at home you understand: call in the experts.

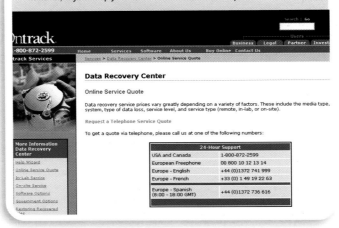

Modern printers typically have a host of configurable options.

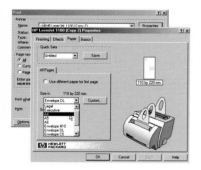

Are paper size and layout settings correct?

Games and other software can play havoc with your display settings so go back to basics. Click Start, point to Settings, click Control Panel, and then double-click Display to access the options.

Printers

Poor print quality? Suspect your choice of paper or some problem with the software settings. Experiment with different paper types and weights and be sure to run any diagnostic program that came with your printer. Also try printing at different resolutions.

Toner If your laser printer's toner is almost exhausted, remove the cartridges and rock it gently from side to side. This re-distributes the remaining toner and may see you through until you can buy a refill. Note that shaking an inkjet's ink cartridges does no good whatsoever.

Inket printheads can move fractionally out of the correct alignment, leading to blurred, bleeding or fuzzy prints. Run the appropriate software utility to fix this.

Blurred Is what you see on screen most definitely *not* what you get on paper? Check that the correct paper size is selected in the print setup settings and be sure to select portrait or landscape views as appropriate.

Paper jams are less common these days than once they were but can still stop a printer dead, particularly if you use a paper type or weight that the printer is not designed to accommodate. Consult the manual for instructions on how to open the unit and extract the mangled sheets.

Modems

Connection Can you hear your modem in action as it dials up your Internet Service Provider (ISP)? Adjust the volume control on an external model until you can hear it chirruping when it tries to make a connection. For an internal modem, click Start, Settings, Control Panel, Modems and adjust the volume in the Properties section of the General tab. So long as you can hear *something*, the modem's not entirely lifeless and the problem is likely to be with the telephone line or, more commonly, a temporary hitch with the ISP.

Has your modem suddenly stopped working? If you've recently added a new extension handset or fax machine somewhere in your house, there may now be too many devices trying to share the same line. Try temporarily unplugging any additions and see if your modem comes back to life.

Diagnostics Try running the Windows diagnostic utility. Click Start, Settings, Control Panel, Modems and select the Diagnostics tab. Highlight your modem and click More Info. Windows now tries to contact the modem and reports back with any problems. 'Port already open' is the most common error message, and invariably means that some software application – perhaps a fax or voice-mail program – is messing up the settings. Close down all running programs and try again.

Pump up the volume to hear if your modem's alive or dead.

Windows will have a stab at rooting out modem troubles.

Are you connected If you *think* that you're online but can't access any websites or send and receive email, make sure that you're really connected. Click Start, click Run, type "winipcfg" (without the quotes), and hit Enter. If you see an IP Address that's not just a string of zeroes, you are indeed online and it's likely that the problem is a glitch with your ISP. If not, your modem is failing to connect. For serious diagnostics, look here (and yes, this does presuppose that you can get online, in which case why do you need a modem trouble-shooter?):
http://support.microsoft.com/support/kb/articles/q142/7/30.asp

An IP address is a guarantee that you're online.

TECHIE CORNER

IRQ-some When hardware devices talk to the rest of the computer, they use one, more or none of the following: Interrupt Request (IRQ), Input/Output address (I/O), Direct Memory Access (DMA) and Memory Address. The first of these, IRQ, frequently leads to conflicts where two devices fight over access to the processor and system resources. Thankfully, Windows can configure most modern "Plug-and-Play" devices (including *all* PCI expansion boards) automatically, but older ISA expansion cards may have hardware jumpers that need to be set correctly.

In the event of a hardware conflict (warning signs: a new peripheral device or expansion card doesn't work or Windows starts freezing and/or crashing inexplicably), get along to Device Manager and look for evidence.
Click Start
Click Settings
Click Control Panel
Click System
Click the Device Manager tab.
Expand the list of hardware by

clicking the + signs and look for anything marked with a yellow (!) – an indication that Windows suspects a problem. Highlight any such devices and click Properties for details.

The most common state of affairs is when two devices try to share a single IRQ. Windows will then prompt you to (temporarily) disable one in order to use the other. This very rapidly becomes a pain, so a better solution by far is to reassign their IRQ addresses. Sounds complicated? Not really – but the precise solution depends on the specific problem. Note too that Windows can share a single IRQ address between certain devices, so just because two pieces of hardware have the same IRQ doesn't necessarily mean that you need to fiddle unless one or the other doesn't work or there's a (!) warning in Device Manager. Look here for a detailed exposition of IRQ and other system resources:
http://www.pcguide.com/ref/ mbsys/res

PART **8**

Appendices

Appendix 1 Upgrade limitations   **144**

Appendix 2 BIOS and CMOS   **145**

Appendix 3 Partitioning your hard disk   **147**

Appendix 4 Glossary   **149**

PART **8**

Appendix 1
Upgrade limitations

Though it pains us to say it, there are times when it's smarter and downright cheaper to toss an ancient PC on the scrap heap (or, better, to donate it to a school or charity) and go buy a new one. Although in theory it's just about possible to upgrade just about everything, computer components are largely interdependent. What this means in practice is that you can't, say, bolt a 30GB hard drive onto a vintage 1994 PC and expect it to work: the BIOS (see p.145) simply won't support it.

Likewise, a system running Windows 3.1 or even Windows 95 can't do a thing with USB, so a new operating system is in order before you even think about adding the like of a USB scanner. But Windows 98 needs 64MB of RAM to run efficiently (32MB at a pinch) and your old PC might have a paltry 8Mb or so onboard. In other words, a memory upgrade might be in order *before* the operating system upgrade that would enable you to add a USB controller card. And even if you do get your system up to speed, does it actually have a free PCI expansion slot? You see the problem...

The pace of hardware development is such that even comparatively modern machines are often unable to cope with an upgrade in one area unless you simultaneously improve various other key components. Say you treat yourself to a camcorder and want to use your computer for video editing. Installing a FireWire expansion card is a good first step, as this enables you to capture the footage onto your PC. But where are you going to store it? Digital film swallows up roughly one gigabyte(!) of disk space per four minutes of footage, so you need a huge hard disk to make it a worthwhile exercise. On top of that, a fast processor (at least a Pentium II) and stacks of RAM are essential unless you have the patience to wait an age for every minor tweak to render on screen. Similarly, adding a DVD drive (even with a decoder card) to a first generation Pentium system isn't going to cut the mustard in the home entertainment stakes.

The bottom line is that it's important to consider the pros and cons of any potential upgrade, check whether your system meets the minimum system requirements, and be realistic about the possibilities.

PART 8

Appendix 2
BIOS and CMOS

Two more dread acronyms! BIOS stands for Basic Input/Output System, and is usually found in the shape of a chip on the motherboard. BIOS kicks in when you first start your PC to get the essential parts of the system – keyboard, monitor, hard disk, ports, etc – up and running before (and independently of) the operating system. Modern BIOSes are Plug-and-Play, which means that they can automatically recognize and configure most new expansion cards and hardware devices. They tend also to be flash upgradeable – i.e. can be updated via an internet download.

The historical trouble with BIOS is that pre-1994 versions couldn't recognize hard disks larger than 528MB; pre-1996 versions managed no more than 2.1GB; and more recent chips gave up at 8.4GB. The good news is that special software (usually supplied with large hard disk drives) can circumvent these infuriating limitations. However, a flash upgrade or even a replacement chip is a better long-term option. If you computer was made by a major manufacturer (Compaq, Dell, HP, IBM), you should be able to download a BIOS upgrade from the Support section of the manufacturer's website. Smaller PC brands require you to find out who made your PC's BIOS. Look for the name during the start-up process – probably Award, Phoenix or AMI – or follow this procedure:
   Click Start
   Click Settings
   Click Control Panel
   Click System
   Click the Device Manager tab.
   Now click the Print button, select System Summary, and click OK. At the very top of the first page to be printed you'll find the BIOS details.

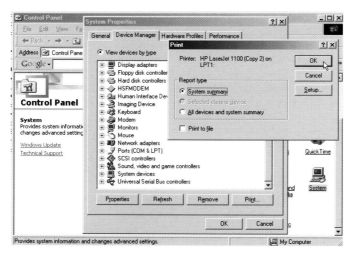

A Device Manager report reveals who made your BIOS. Check the manufacturer's website for further details.

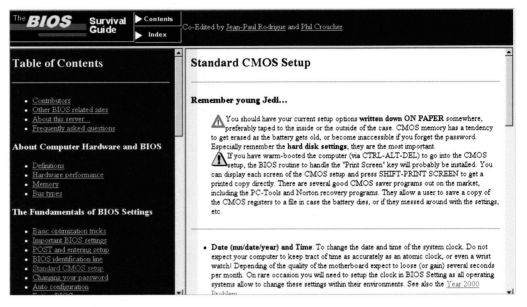

The BIOS Survival Guide — Co-Edited by Jean-Paul Rodrigue and Phil Croucher

Table of Contents

- Contributors
- Other BIOS related sites
- About this server...
- Frequently asked questions

About Computer Hardware and BIOS

- Definitions
- Hardware performance
- Memory
- Bus types

The Fundamentals of BIOS Settings

- Basic optimization tricks
- Important BIOS settings
- POST and entering setup
- BIOS identification line
- Standard CMOS setup
- Changing your password
- Auto configuration

Standard CMOS Setup

Remember young Jedi...

⚠ You should have your current setup options **written down ON PAPER** somewhere, preferably taped to the inside or the outside of the case. CMOS memory has a tendency to get erased as the battery gets old, or become inaccessible if you forget the password. Especially remember the **hard disk settings**; they are the most important.

⚠ If you have warm-booted the computer (via CTRL-ALT-DEL) to go into the CMOS setup, the BIOS routine to handle the "Print Screen" key will probably be installed. You can display each screen of the CMOS setup and press SHIFT-PRINT SCREEN to get a printed copy directly. There are several good CMOS saver programs out on the market, including the PC-Tools and Norton recovery programs. They allow a user to save a copy of the CMOS registers to a file in case the battery dies, or if they messed around with the settings, etc.

- **Date (mn/date/year) and Time**: To change the date and time of the system clock. Do not expect your computer to keep tract of time as accurately as an atomic clock, or even a wrist watch! Depending on the quality of the motherboard expect to loose (or gain) several seconds per month. On rare occasion you will need to setup the clock in BIOS Setting as all operating systems allow to change these settings within their environments. See also the Year 2000 Problem.

A pencil and paper (remember them?) come in handy for making a record of CMOS settings.

CMOS means Complementary Metal-Oxide Semiconductor. This is essentially a form of permanent memory powered by a battery that keeps a record of your system's configuration when the power is off. Here you might change details about, for instance, the drive order in which your PC tries to boot (usually floppy drive followed by the hard disk), power management settings, port configuration and BIOS settings.

Doesn't sound like much fun, does it? Truth to tell you might never need to go near CMOS. However, should the battery ever fail or something else go seriously awry, a written copy of your CMOS setup would prove invaluable. Now would be a very good time to make just such a document.

To access CMOS, look for onscreen instructions next time you switch on your PC (usually "Press Del to enter Setup" or press the F2 key or similar). You'll find instructions on screen on how to navigate using the keyboard, so go to the CMOS pages and write down everything you see. Be sure to accurately note all details pertaining to your computer's disk drives, especially capacity, cylinders, heads, landing zone (don't ask), sectors and anything else you can see. When you're through, press the Escape key until you're back at the start page and confirm that you want to exit without making any changes. Windows will now start as normal.

For more on this stuff, check the excellent BIOS survival guide here: **http://burks.bton.ac.uk/burks/pcinfo/hardware/bios_sg/bios_sg.htm**

Appendix 3
Partitioning your hard disk

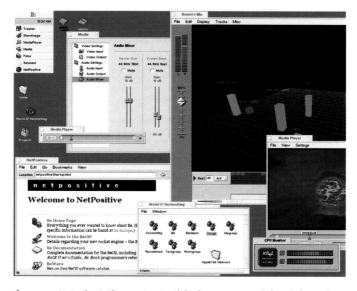

As we stated at the outset, this is a manual for PC owners, not the Mac brigade. But more than this, we have been dealing exclusively with the Windows-based systems. But there *are* alternatives out there, notably the free (via download; otherwise inexpensive in boxed form) and open source Linux. The problem with Linux is that it's just not suitable for non-experts. It's powerful, fast, endlessly flexible and stable – but it's a nightmare to set up and, despite a choice of bolt-on graphical interfaces, it remains at heart a text-based system.

There's also an operating system called BeOS. This one is optimized for multimedia performance but suffers badly from lack of hardware support (i.e. hardware manufacturers don't bother writing drivers to make their device work with BeOS because, um, nobody uses it yet. Chicken-and-egg, anyone?). See **http://www.linux.org** and **http://www.be.com/products/freebeos** for more information.

Now, we'd be the first to encourage people to experiment with alternative operating systems, but don't throw out the baby with the bath water. Rather, it makes much more sense to install the secondary operating system alongside Windows on the same system. The trick lies in creating disk partitions, which effectively

Linux can look any way you want it to. It can even look a little like Windows.

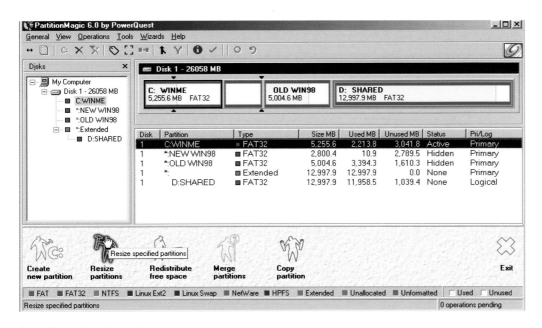

A partitioned hard disk looks and behaves for all the world like two or more distinct computers.

splits a hard disk into two or more independent sections. Each operating system can then be installed into a different partition as if it was a physically distinct hard disk. When you start your computer, you simply choose which system you want to work with.

Indeed, we'd recommend this when upgrading from one version of Windows to another: make sure that you're happy with your new toy before making a wholesale change.

Windows comes with its own partitioning utility called Fdisk. However, as Microsoft points out: "you should not use this tool unless you are very familiar with the process of partitioning a hard disk." Quite. It's much, much easier – and a good deal safer – to purchase a specialized program like Partition Magic from PowerQuest (**http://www.powerquest.com/partitionmagic**). Even here, the process is not exactly intuitive – you'll need to learn a little about the language of file systems and logical, primary and extended partitions and the like – but at least you get to work in the graphical environment of Windows rather than the scary old world of DOS. Partition Magic also lets you dynamically resize partitions without loss of data, something that Fdisk alone can't manage.

Oh, one more thing: always make a *complete* back up of all your files before attempting work on your hard disk. Data loss is a remote but nonetheless real possibility.

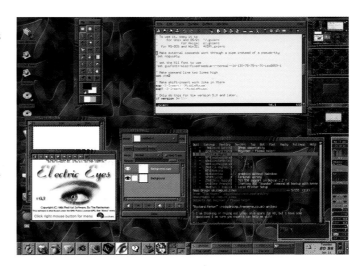

The BeOS operating system is ideal for multimedia work but it's not the best choice for the average domestic desktop.

PART 8

Appendix 4
Glossary

Here's an at-a-glance guide to many of the techie terms used throughout this manual, along with several more that you'll doubtless come across on your travels around the mind-numbing world of computer jargon. Always remember: if in doubt about what something means, just ask (at which point you'll invariably find that the salesperson so keen to take your money doesn't really have a clue either!).

Let's start with a table of the storage units used in computer-speak.

Name	Symbol	Size
Bit	b	A single binary unit i.e. a 1 or a 0
Byte	B	8 bits
Kilobit	Kb	1,024 bits (= 128 bytes)
Kilobyte	KB	1,024 bytes
Megabit	Mb	1,048,576 bits (=131,072 bytes)
Megabyte	MB	1,048,576 bytes (= 1,024 kilobytes)
Gigabyte	GB	1,073,741,824 bytes (= 1,024 megabytes)

A hard disk.

286/386/486 Early processors from Intel used to power desktop computers. Eventually superseded by the Pentium processor

56,000bps/56Kbps The theoretical top speed of modern modems i.e. capable of receiving up to 56,000 bits of data per second

AGP Accelerated Graphics Port. A computer interface (usually a slot on the motherboard) designed for a high performance graphics display

Analog A continuous signal

Anti-virus software A program designed to protect a computer from malicious viruses

ATAPI Advanced Technology Attachment Packet Interface. An interface for connecting disk drives to a computer

ADF Automatic Document Feeder. An attachment for scanners and printers that enables multiple sheets to be processed without manual intervention

Backup A copy of vital computer files made for safekeeping

Bandwidth A measure of how much data can be transferred through a channel at any one time

BIOS Basic Input/Output System. Software stored in a chip that controls the operation of a computer at its most fundamental level

A BIOS chip.

Blanking plates Removable covers on a computer case that protect unused expansion slots

Bus A path on a motherboard (or cable) through which data can pass

CRT Cathode Ray Tube. The glass tube used to produce an image in a television set and some computer monitors

CD-ROM A version of the compact disc that holds computer data. CD-R (Recordable) and CD-RW (Rewritable) formats are blank discs on which files may be saved with a CD writer driver

A motherboard bus.

Celeron A slower but cheaper version of the Pentium processor

Chipset Integrated circuits on the motherboard that provide support for the microprocessor, memory and expansion slots

Clock speed The rate at which a computer's processor operates, expressed in Megahertz or Gigahertz

CMOS Complementary Metal-Oxide Semiconductor. A fabrication technology used by the chip that remembers basic system settings

Color depth A measure of how many colors a monitor can display. 1-bit color is black and white; 24-bit color is up to 16.7 million distinct hues

COM port Communications port. A connector for devices like mice and modems

A CRT monitor.

Control panel An area in Windows where you can configure your PC

CPU Central Processing Unit. The main system processor

Crash When the computer errs and stops working!

Cursor An arrow on the screen controlled by the mouse, or an insertion point in a document

Defragment To reorganize files that have become split up and are stored piecemeal on the hard disk

Desktop The main screen within Windows before you launch any programs. The Desktop is home to icons like My Computer and the Recycle Bin

Dial-up Networking The program Windows uses to connect a computer to the internet through a phone line

Digital In contrast to analog, a digital signal is information encoded as different states of the signal (usually a series of on/off signals)

Defragmenting a hard disk.

DOS Disk Operating System. A text-based operating system for PCs developed by Microsoft. DOS was the precursor to Windows

Dot pitch The distance between the tiny dots of a single color on a monitor screen that together make up a picture

DPI Dots Per Inch. A measure of an image's resolution. The higher the DPI, the greater the clarity

Download The process of acquiring a file onto your PC from the internet

Drive A machine that reads data from and writes data to a disk or tape

Drive bay A space in a computer reserved for a drive

Driver A software program that lets the operating system 'talk' to and control a device

DVD Digital Versatile Disc. A Compact Disc-derivative capable of storing a huge amount of data, including movies

e

EIDE Enhanced Integrated Drive Electronics. An interface for connecting devices like the hard disk to a computer

EPP Enhanced Parallel Port. The modern, fast version of the parallel port used to connect a printer (a replacement for the slower Centronics standard)

Expansion card A circuit board that can be added to a computer to enhance its capabilities

An expansion card.

Expansion slot An interface on a motherboard used to connect an expansion card

f

Firewall A program or hardware device that aims to protect a computer against unauthorized access, particularly by hackers

Flatbed A type of scanner that uses a flat glass plate, much like a photocopier

Floppy disk A non-floppy plastic square that holds up to 1.44MB of data (okay, it's floppy on the *inside!*)

Format To format a disk is to make it useable in a certain type of drive

g

Full duplex The ability to send and receive data simultaneously

Graphics card The circuitry in a computer that controls the monitor display, usually in the form of an expansion card. Sometimes called a video card

h

Hard disk A magnetic disk on which may be stored a great deal of data, including a computer's operating system

Hardware The physical components that make up a computer system

i

Icon A small clickable image that denotes a file or application within Windows

Inkjet printer A device that squirts wet ink onto paper in order to print text and images

Interface The look and feel of a software program; or the means by which computer components communicate

An inkjet printer.

IRQ Interrupt Request. One of the means by which hardware devices gain the processor's attention

ISA Industry Standard Architecture. The oldest type of expansion slot still found in PCs

Jaz drive A high-capacity removable hard disk storage device made by Iomega

Joystick A device for controlling the action in computer games

Jumpers Small pins that control the settings on drives and motherboards

Jumpers on a drive

Laser printer A device that uses dry toner and laser light to print text and images

LCD Liquid Crystal Display. The technology used in flat-panel monitors

MIDI Musical Instrument Digital Interface. A means of connecting electronic musical instruments to a computer

An external modem.

Modem A device that enables a computer to use the telephone line in order to communicate with other computers in a network, especially the internet

Motherboard The central circuit board in a computer to which all other devices are attached

Multimedia Loosely speaking, the combination of text, sound and video. Most CD-ROMs are multimedia, as are many websites

Notebook A portable computer.
Used to be called a laptop

OEM Original Equipment Manufacturer. This refers to computer components sold directly and exclusively to manufacturers i.e. not available to the public

Operating system Software that governs the workings of a computer, both in terms of hardware and applications

Partition A sub-division of a hard disk that the computer treats just like a separate hard disk

PCI Peripheral Component Interconnect. An expansion slot standard, faster and more flexible than ISA

Pentium A family of powerful microprocessors developed by Intel

Plug-and-Play A standard that enables a Windows-based PC to automatically recognize and configure any new device

Port An external socket used to connect devices to a computer

Processor A silicon chip that processes data. Effectively, your PC's brain

Program A set of instructions that enables a computer to perform certain tasks. One example would be a word processor

Plug it in and play straight away.

QWERTY The standard layout of the keys on a computer keyboard, where the first 6 letters on the top row are Q,W,E,R,T and Y

Resolution A measure of the level of detail in an image on either a monitor screen or printed page

RAM Random Access Memory. Dynamic memory used by a PC as its working space

Registry A Windows' database with information on all hardware and software that together comprises the PC system

ROM Read Only Memory. As in a BIOS chip or CD-ROM, this is a form of memory used for data storage that can be accessed (read) but not changed (written)

A RAM module.

Scanner A device that uses a light sensor to convert printed documents into data which can then be interpreted by software on a computer

SCSI Small Computer System Interface. A fast interface used to connect devices to a computer

Serial port A port on the back of a PC used to connect devices like mice and modems

Software Computer programs, including application software like a spreadsheet program and operating systems like Windows

A scanner.

Swap file An area of the hard disk used by Windows as 'virtual memory', or surrogate RAM

Taskbar A bar running along the bottom of the screen in Windows that shows which programs are running and lets you select between them with buttons

Twain The software interface standard that enables scanners to work with imaging software

USB Universal Serial Bus. A relatively fast interface with which peripherals can easily connect to a computer

Upgrade To improve, enhance or modify the performance of your computer

V.90/V.92 Communications standards that modern modems adhere to

VGA Video Graphics Array. A basic standard governing monitor displays (16 colours at a resolution of 640 x 480)

USB connectors.

Video card *See graphics card*

Virus A malicious computer program, usually spread on disk or over the internet

WYSIWYG What You See Is What You Get. This means that the image you see on your monitor is exactly what comes out of your printer

Zip drive A high-capacity floppy disk storage device made by Iomega

Index

3D-audio 81
3D-graphics cards 78

abacuses 12
Add/Remove Programs 120-1
ADFs (Automatic Document
Feeders), scanners 111, 112
AGP
(Accelerated Graphics Port)
expansion slots 74-5
graphics cards 43, 77
Allen, Paul 13
Altair 8800 computer 13
AMD processors 18, 22,
23, 37
AMR (Audio Modem Riser)
expansion slots 75
analogue v digital monitors 96
Analytical Engine,
Babbage's 12
antistatic wrist straps 32, 33,
78, 82
API (Application Programming
Interface) standard 77
appendices 143-53
BIOS and CMOS 145-6
glossary 149-53
partitioning, hard disk 147-8
upgrade limitations 144
Apple Computers 7, 13
application software,
described 11
architecture
expansion cards and 74-5
motherboards and 74-5
ARPANet (Advanced Research
Projects Agency network) 12
Atanasoff, John Vincent 12
ATAPI (Advanced Technology
Attachment Packet Interface)
standard 51, 62-3
audio

3D 81
cables 82-3
CDs 63
connectors 17, 63, 67
see also sound; sound cards;
speakers

Babbage, Charles 12
backup
data 26-30, 53, 70
startup disks 26-8
bays, drive see drive bays
BeOS operating system 147,
148
Berners-Lee, Tim 13
Berry, Clifford 12
Bezos, Jeff 13
binary code 39
BIOS (Basic Input/Output
System) 43, 145-6
DVD drive upgrading 67
flash upgrades 145
hard disk upgrading 55
inventory 24
processor upgrading 38, 41
bits, and buses 75
boosting performance 35-47
motherboards 42-3
processors 36-41
RAM 44-7
upgrade reason 14
boot disks 27-8
booting, cold/warm 129
broadband Internet access 85
buffers, CD-RW 63
buses, and bits 75

cables
audio 82-3
power, splitters 56
USB 89, 137
capacitive keyboards 98

cartridges, inkjet 140
cases, PC 16
inventory 24
opening 33
CD-ROM drivers 28
CD-ROM drives
CD-R (recordable) drives
58-9, 60, 61
CD-ROM (read-only
memory) drives 59
CD-RW (rewriteable) drives
29, 59-63
cleaning 138
described 16, 19
inventory 24
recordable 58-63
speed 61
trouble-shooting 63, 138
upgrading 58-63
CD-ROMs
capacity 59
problem 138
recordable 29, 58-63
see also CD-ROM drives
Celeron processors 37
channels 50-1
chipset, performance 38
cleaning, PC 130-3
Cleanup, Disk 118
CMOS (Complementary Metal-
Oxide Semiconductor) 145
batteries 43
hard disk upgrading 55, 57
CNR (Communications
and Networking Riser)
expansion slots 75
Colossus computer 12
compact discs see CD-ROM
drives; CD-ROMs
compatibility, motherboards/
processors 38, 41
conflicts, hardware 137
IRQs 141
modems 140
sound cards 83
connectors
audio 17, 63, 67
graphics cards 78

keyboards 97
modems 17
monitors 17
peripherals 17
processors 37
sound cards 81
consumables, printer 106
cooling, processors 38, 40,
41, 78
cooling fans 17
cleaning 131
cordless mice 101
crash protection 123,
138, 139
CRT (Cathode Ray Tube)
monitors 92-6
Cyrix processors 18, 37

data recovery, hard disks 139
DDR (Double Date Rate)
RAM 44
DEC (Digital Equipment
Corporation) 12
decoder cards, DVD drives
65, 66-7
defragmenting 15, 116
degaussing, monitors
127, 139
device advice 22
Device Manager, Windows
22, 24-5
Difference Engine,
Babbage's 12
digital v analogue monitors 96
digital speakers 103
digital video 76
DIMMS (Dual Inline Memory
Modules), RAM 24, 43,
44, 45, 46-7
Direct3D games standard 77
Disk Cleanup 118
disk defragmenting 15, 116
disk imaging 123
display settings,
graphics cards 79

distortion, monitors 93
DMA (Direct Memory Access) 55, 141
DOS (Microsoft Disk Operating System, MS-DOS) 27
DOS partitions 57
drive bays
    CD drives 62-3
    described 19, 55
    inventory 25
Drive Converter 119
drive letters, inventory 25
drivers, software 28, 79, 86, 109, 136
drives
    adding new 49-71
    external 70-1
DSL (Digital Subscriber Line) Internet access 85
duplex sound cards 81
DVD (digital video/versatile disc) drives
    adding 64-7
    decoder cards 65, 66-7
    home cinema 64-5
    inventory 25
    masters/slaves 66
    recordable 65
    regional coding 66, 139
    speed 65
    trouble-shooting 66, 67, 139
    upgrading 66-7

'Easy PC' 15
Eckert, John Presper 12
EIDE (Enhanced Integrated Drive Electronics) standard 51, 55
electricity
electrical storms 127
    magnetism 126-7, 139
    safety 32, 33, 130, 133
    spikes 127
    static 32, 33, 131, 133
    see also power

emergency disks 26-8
encryption 123
enhancing, upgrade reason 14
ENIAC (Electronic Numerical Integrator and Computer) 12
ergonomic keyboards 97-8
expansion cards 73-89
    and architecture 74-5
    cleaning 133
    graphics cards 76-9
    modems 84-6
    sound cards 80-3
    USBs 87-9
expansion slots
    described 18, 43
    inventory 25
    standards 74-5, 77, 81
external
    drives 70-1
    hard disks 52-3
    modems 84, 86

FAT 32 (File Allocation Table)
    file system converting to 119
    hard disk upgrading 57
fax modems 85
Fdisk utility 148
features, adding 14
file recovery 123
firewalls 123
FireWire devices 15, 62, 70, 87, 88
flash upgrades, BIOS 145
flashlight 32
flat panel, monitor 92
flatbed scanners 110-11
flickering, monitors 139
floppy disks
    emergency 26-8
    first 13
floppy drives
    described 16, 19
    inventory 24
    replacing 68-9
    sockets 43

formatting hard disks 57
FST (Flat Square Tube) monitors 93
functionality, adding 14

games and gaming 76-7, 140
Gates, Bill 13
glossary 149-53
GPU (Graphics Processing Unit) 78
graphics cards
    3D-graphics cards 78
    AGP slots 43, 74-5, 77
    connectors, external 78
    described 18
    display settings 79
    DVD 65, 67
    interfaces 77
    inventory 25
    memory 77
    refresh rates 78, 139
    resolution 76-7, 93
    trouble-shooting 78, 95, 139-40
    upgrading 37, 76-9
    see also monitors
graphics tablets 21

hard disks
    capacity 54
    data recovery 139
    described 19
    disasters 139
    external 52-3
    FAT 32 file system 57, 119
    first 13
    formatting 57
    interfaces 24, 43
    internal 54-7
    inventory 24
    jumpers 56, 63
    masters/slaves 56

noises, unexpected 138
    partitioning 57, 147-8
    setup software 55
    size 55
    speed 54-5
    trouble-shooting 138, 139
    upgrading 52-7
hardware
    components 11
    conflicts see conflicts, hardware
    hardware acceleration, DVD drives 65
help lines,
    technical support 129
history,
    personal computing 10-13
Hollerith, Hermann 12
home cinema
    DVD 64-5
    speakers 103
host adapters 50-1
housekeeping 29-30

I/O (Input/Output) address 141
    see also BIOS
IBM International Business Machines), origin 12
IDE (Integrated Drive Electronics)
    CD-RW drive upgrade 62-3
    controllers 24, 43, 50-1, 70
    secondary hard disks 56
    standards 51
imaging, disk 123
inkjet cartridges 140
inside explained 18-19
integrated circuits 12
integration,
    motherboards 15, 75
Intel company 14
Intel processors 18, 23, 37, 39
interfaces
    described 17

drives 50-1, 62
DVD 65
graphics cards 77
hard disk 24, 43
printers 105
scanners 111
SCSI 24, 51, 62, 87
USB 88
Internet
  broadband access 85
  connection diagnostics
    140-1
  origins 12, 13
inventory, making an 24-5
IRQs (Interrupt Requests),
  hardware conflicts 141
ISA (Industry Standard
  Architecture) expansion slots
  74-5, 81

Jaz drives 53, 70
Jobs, Steve 13
joysticks
  described 21
  inventory 25
jumpers (switches)
  CD drives 63
  DVD drives 66
  hard disks 56, 63
  motherboards 41

keyboards
  capacitive 98
  cleaning 132
  connectors 97
  described 20
  ergonomic 97-8
  installing 99
  MIDI 21
  switch-based 98
  trackballs, integral 98
  trouble-shooting 99
  USB 99

LCD (Liquid Crystal Display)
  monitors 92-6
Leibnitz, Gottfried von 12
lids, lifting 33
lightning 127
limitations, upgrade 144
Linux operating system 147
LS-120 SuperDisk drives 69

Mac computers 7, 13
macro viruses 125
magnetism 126-7, 139
maintenance, PC 114-33
Maintenance Wizard 119
manuals 32, 33, 41, 137
manufacturer/model,
  inventory 24
masters/slaves
  CD-RW drives 63
  DVD drives 66
  hard disks 56
Mauchly, John 12
media, printers 107
memory
  CMOS 146
  DMA 55, 141
  graphics cards 77
  printers 106
  RAM see RAM
mice
  cleaning 132
  cordless 101
  described 21
  optical 101
  sockets 43
  trouble-shooting 101
  upgrading 100-1
Microsoft Backup 30
Microsoft company 13
Microsoft Disk Operating
  System (MS-DOS) 27
MIDI (Musical Instrument

Digital Interface) 81
  keyboards 21
'minimum system
  requirements' 22
modems
  choosing 86
  conflicts 140
  connectors 17
  described 21
  diagnostics 84, 140-1
  drivers 86
  external/internal 84, 86
  fax modems 85
  installing 84
  inventory 25
  software 86
  speed 85, 86
  trouble-shooting 86, 140-1
  upgrading 84-6
  V.90/V.92 standard 85
  voice-enabled 86
monitors
  cleaning 131
  connectors 17
  CRT/LCD 92-6
  degaussing 127, 139
  described 20
  digital v analogue 96
  dimensions 94
  dismantling (not) 133
  distortion 93
  dual 96
  flat panel 92
  flickering 139
  FST 93
  installing 95
  inventory 25
  price 94
  refresh rates 93, 94, 139
  resolution 76-7, 93
  screen size 92
  trouble-shooting 78, 95,
    139-40
  tweaking 95
  upgrading 92-6
  viewing angle 94
  see also graphics cards
Moore, Gordon 14

motherboards and architecture
  74-5
  described 19
  integration 15, 75
  jumpers 41
  manuals 32, 41
  processors compatibility 38,
    41
  upgrading 42-3
mouse see mice
MOVs (metal-oxide varistors),
  power surge protection 127
MP3 file format 80
MPEG-2 video 65
MS-DOS (Microsoft Disk
  Operating System) 27
multifunction devices,
  peripherals 108
music see MIDI

OCR (Optical Character
  Recognition) packages,
  scanners 112
on/off switches 16
OpenGL games standard 77
opening PC cases 33
operating systems
  BeOS 147, 148
  described 11
  inventory 24
  Linux 147
  MS-DOS 27
  UNIX 13
  Windows see Windows
optical drives/media 60
  trouble-shooting 138-9
  see also CD-ROM drives;
  CD-ROMs
optical mice 101
outages, power 128-9
outside explained 16-17

p

'packet writing' software 59-60
PalmPilot palmtop
    computers 13
parallel ports 17, 43
partitioning, hard disk 57,
    147-8
Partition Magic 148
Pascal, Blaise (1623-1662)
    11, 12
patience 32
PC cleaning 130-3
PC maintenance 114-33
PCI (Peripheral Component
    Interconnect) expansion slots
    74-5, 77, 81
PDP-8 computer 12
Pentium processors 37, 39
performance, boosting see
    boosting performance
peripherals 91-113
    cleaning 133
    connectors 17
    explained 20-1
    inventory 25
    keyboards 97-9
    mice 100-1
    monitors 92-6
    printers 104-9
    scanners 110-13
    speakers 102-3
'plug and play', USB 88
power
    cables, splitters 56
    checking 136
    on/off 129
    outages 128-9
    saving 129
    supply, described 18
    surges 127
    switches 17
    see also electricity
precautions, taking 26-30,
    126-9
printers
    consumables 106

described 21
duty cycle 108
installing 109
interface 105
inventory 25
lifespan 108
media 107
memory 106
multifunction devices 108
resolution 106
software 108
speed 107
technologies 107
toner 140
trouble-shooting 109, 140
upgrading 104-9
USB 105
processors
    AMD 18, 22, 23, 37
    boosting performance 36-41
    Celeron 37
    connectors 37
    cooling 38, 40, 41, 78
    Cyrix 18, 37
    described 18, 22, 23
    Intel 18, 23, 37, 39
    inventory 24
    motherboard compatibility
        38, 41
    Pentium 37, 39
    speed 24, 39
    upgrading 36-41
PS/2-type ports 17
punched cards 12

r

RAM (Random Access
    Memory)
    DDR 44
    described 19
    determining 22
    DIMMS 24, 43, 44, 45,
        46-7
    inventory 24
    problem symptoms 138
    RD 44

RIMMS 46
SIMMS 24, 44-5, 46, 47
speed 45
trouble-shooting 47
types 44-5
upgrading 37, 43, 44-7
RD (Rambus Dynamic) RAM
    44
reading/writing
    CD-ROMs 29, 59-63
    hard disk 19
recovering data 139
refresh rates
    graphics cards 78, 139
    monitors 93, 94, 139
regional coding, DVD drives
    66, 139
repairing, upgrade reason 14
rescue disks 26-8
reset switches 16
resolution
    graphics cards 76-7, 93
    monitors 76-7, 93
    printers 106
    scanners 111
RIMMs (Rambus Inline
    Memory Modules) 46
RJ-11 sockets 17
RJ-45 sockets 17
rooting around 23
RSI (Repetitive Strain Injury)
    97, 98

s

safety, electrical 32, 33, 130,
    133
sampling, sound 82
SANDRA (System ANalyser,
    Diagnostic and Reporting
    Assistant) 23, 24-5, 32
satellites (speakers) 102
ScanDisk 117
scanners
    ADFs 111, 112
    cleaning 133
    described 20

flatbed 110-11
handheld 110, 111
installing 113
interface 111
inventory 25
OCR packages 112
pen-sized 110, 111
resolution 111
software 112
speed 112
trouble-shooting 113
TWAIN standard 112
types 110-11
upgrading 110-13
USB 113
screens 92
screens see monitors
screwdrivers 32
script viruses 125
SCSI (Small Computer Systems
    Interface), controllers 24,
    51, 62, 87
SD (Synchronous Dynamic)
    RAM 44
serial number, inventory 24
serial ports 17, 43
SIMMS (Single Inline Memory
    Modules), RAM 24, 44-5,
    46, 47
Sinclair, Clive 13
software
    applications 11
    drivers 28, 79, 86, 109,
        136
    DVD 65
    modems 86
    'packet writing' 59-60
    printers 108
    scanners 112
    utilities 23
sound
    sampling 82
    surround 102
    sound cards
        conflicts 83
        connectors 81
        described 18
        duplex 81

DVD 65, 67
  inventory 25
  trouble-shooting 83, 138
  upgrading 80-3
  see also speakers
speakers 81
  described 20
  digital 103
  DVD drive upgrade 67
  home cinema 103
  installing 103
  inventory 25
  trouble-shooting 83, 138
  upgrading 102-3
  USB 103
  see also sound cards
speed
  CD-ROM drives 61
  DVD drives 65
  hard disks 54-5
  modems 85, 86
  printers 107
  processors 24, 39
  RAM 45
  scanners 112
  system bus 38, 39, 41
  USB 88
speed trap 23
spikes, electrical 127
splitters, power cables 56
startup disks, Windows 27-8
static electricity 32, 33, 131,
  133
stock, taking 22-3
subwoofers (speakers) 102
surges, power 127
surround sound 102
SVGA (Super Video Graphics
  Array) resolution 76-7
switch-based keyboards 98
System ANalyser, Diagnostic
  and Reporting Assistant
  (SANDRA) 23, 24-5, 32
  system bus speed 38
  multiplier 39, 41
  System Information tool,
  Windows 23
  System Restore utility 137

taking stock 22-3
tape drives 53
technical support help lines
  129
third party utilities 122-3
timeline, history 12-13
toner, printers 140
tools 31-2
trackballs 101
  keyboard 98
trojan viruses 125
trouble-shooting 135-41
  CD-ROM drives 63, 138
  DVD drives 66, 67, 139
  general 136-7
  graphics cards 78, 95, 139-
  40
  hard disks 138, 139
  keyboards 99
  mice 101
  modems 86, 140-1
  monitors 78, 95, 139-40
  optical drives 138-9
  printers 109, 140
  RAM 47
  scanners 113
  sound cards 83, 138
  speakers 83, 138
  specific problems 138-41
  USB 89
Turing, Alan 12
TWAIN (Technology Without
  An Interesting Name)
  standard, scanners 112
tweezers 32

uninstalling programs 120-1,
  123
UNIVAC (Universal Automatic
  Computer) 12
UNIX operating system 13
upgrading
  interdependence 144

  limitations 144
  reasons 14-15
  types 14
  see also named components
UPS (Uninterruptible Power
  Supply) 128
US Robotics 13
USB (Universal Serial Bus)
  adding 87-9
  cables 89, 137
  interface 88
  keyboards 99
  ports 17, 43
  scanners 113
  speakers 103
  speed 88
  trouble-shooting 89
  Windows compatibility 87
utilities
  software 23
  third party 122-3
  Windows 116-21, 137, 148

V.90/V.92 standard, modems
  85
viruses 124-5
voice-enabled modems 86

WAV (wave table) 81, 83
web services, utilities 123
webcams 21
websites
  AGP expansion slots 75
  audio CDs 63
  backup 30
  BeOS 147
  BIOS 146
  CD technology 60, 63
  drivers 28
  DVD technology 67
  floppy disk drives 69
  gaming 77
  graphics cards 79

  hard disk upgrading 57
  Internet access 85
  IRQs 141
  memory 47
  modems 141
  monitors 93, 96
  processor upgrading 41
  sound 81, 103
  speakers 103
  trouble-shooting 137
  USB 87
  V.92 modem standard 85
  viruses 124, 125
Winchester hard disks 13
Windows 95
  Microsoft Backup 30
  original cf later 57, 87
  startup disk 28
  USB compatibility 87
Windows 98
  Microsoft Backup 30
  startup disk 27
  USB compatibility 87
Windows
  first 13
  utilities 116-21, 137, 148
WinZip 123
World Wide Web, origins 13
worm viruses 125
Wozniak, Steve 13
wrist straps, antistatic 32, 33,
  78, 82
writing/reading
  CD-ROMs 29, 59-63
  hard disk 19

ZIF (Zero Insertion Force)
  39, 41
Zip drives
  connectivity 88
  data backup 29, 53, 70
  inventory 25
zip utility 123
ZX Spectrum computer 13
ZX-80 computer 13